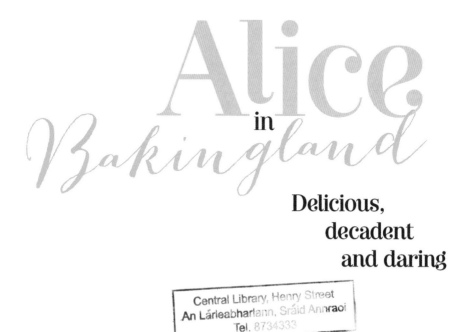

Alice in Bakingland

Delicious, decadent and daring

Alice Arndell

Photography by Murray Lloyd

HarperCollinsPublishers

For my favourite 'big person'
and my favourite 'little person'.
I love you both lots and lotsa.

500 ML

ARTISAN

Model 5KSM150
220-240V   50/60 Hz
300W, 10 min.   App.No. N15779
Made in USA

HarperCollins*Publishers*

First published in 2013
by HarperCollins*Publishers (New Zealand) Limited*
PO Box 1, Shortland Street, Auckland 1140

HarperCollins*Publishers*
31 View Road, Glenfield, Auckland 0627, New Zealand
Level 13, 201 Elizabeth Street, Sydney, NSW 2000, Australia
A 53, Sector 57, Noida, UP, India
77–85 Fulham Palace Road, London W6 8JB, United Kingdom
2 Bloor Street East, 20th floor, Toronto, Ontario M4W 1A8, Canada
10 East 53rd Street, New York, NY 10022, USA

National Library of New Zealand Cataloguing-in-Publication Data
Arndell, Alice.
Alice in Bakingland / Alice Arndell.
Includes index.
ISBN 978-1-77554-015-1
1. Baking. I. Title.
641.815—dc 23

ISBN: 978 1 77554 015 1

Cover and internal design by Cheryl Rowe
Photography by Murray Lloyd
Publisher: Vicki Marsdon
Project Editor: Antoinette Sturny
Printed by RR Donnelley, China, on 157gsm Matt Art

Contents

Introduction

There is something incredibly meaningful and touching about someone presenting you with something they've made with their own hands. Whether it is a simple biscuit or the most elaborate layer cake, everything about home baking and what it means comes down to us showing others how much we care by putting time and effort into something that exists only for a fleeting moment before it's consumed by eager hands and mouths.

These days bakers come in all shapes and sizes and from all walks of life — as television programmes like *Chelsea New Zealand's Hottest Home Baker* show us. Some live in cities with access to an amazing array of ingredients and tools. Others, like me, live in small country towns where only basic supermarket ingredients are to hand. Some are taught by their grandmothers or mothers, others by recipe books and the internet.

With the recent resurgence of home baking I want this book to celebrate what it means to be a home baker. To show you that you don't need fancy equipment or expensive ingredients to make delicious food. Most of all, I want to show you that anyone can do it, that being self-taught (like I am) isn't an impediment to baking and that all you need is a little time, patience, practice and the right recipe. And once you've mastered the basics, the sky-high pavlova is the limit as you begin to experiment with your own flavour combinations and recipe creations.

Each of the recipes in this book has been developed by a home baker, in a home kitchen — the majority using supermarket-sourced ingredients. No fancy equipment or specialty ingredients in the cupboard; just good old-fashioned home baking at its best.

When I set out to write this book I wanted it to be for someone like me. Someone who bakes for their family and friends. Someone who bakes to fill the tins and satisfy a sweet tooth. Someone who bakes to save a few pennies or make healthier choices. Someone who bakes as a creative outlet or as an outlet for stress relief. Someone who bakes for special occasions, bakes every day or bakes just for the fun of it. Someone who bakes to spread a little happiness and joy. Someone who bakes to share love. In other words, I set out to write this book for a home baker.

I hope you relish filling your home with the smells and tastes of delicious home baking as much as I do.

Enjoy!

Alice

Delicious

Simple but never boring — each of the recipes in this chapter
has been carefully chosen to show you just what can be done
with basic store-cupboard and supermarket-sourced ingredients
and a minimum of equipment. A few mixing bowls, a couple of
different cake tins, an electric beater and measuring equipment
are pretty much all you need to bake delicious treats for your
friends and family.

Raspberry *Rings*

Delicious, delicate and reminiscent of childhood, these crisp little biscuits sandwiched with raspberry jam and sprinkled with icing sugar are great for a proper grown-up afternoon tea.

Makes about 24 rings

200 g butter, softened
½ cup sugar
4 tbsp sweetened condensed milk
2 tbsp milk
2 cups plain flour

2 tsp baking powder
¼ tsp salt
raspberry jam (see page 46)
icing sugar

1   Cream butter and sugar until light and fluffy. Beat in condensed milk.

2   Add milk, flour, baking powder and salt and stir until combined.

3   Shape dough into two flat discs, wrap in plastic wrap and refrigerate for at least 30 minutes.

4   Preheat oven to 190°C. Line baking trays with baking paper.

5   Remove one disc of dough from the fridge and roll out on a very well floured bench to about 4 mm thick. Cut out 5 cm rounds and place on baking trays. Cut small shapes out of the middle of half the rounds (these will be the 'tops' of the rings). Return unused dough to the fridge to firm up again and use the second disc of dough to cut out more rounds.

6   Bake for 8–12 minutes or until just starting to go brown around the edges. Cool on a wire rack.

7   Once biscuits are cold, sandwich together a 'top' and a 'bottom' with a generous teaspoon of raspberry jam, and dust lightly with icing sugar.

Variation
Use any flavour of jam you like for these biscuits. You could also use a citrus curd, and perhaps add one tablespoon of poppy seeds to the dough for extra crunch.

Oaty Apricot and Chocolate *Cookies*

These cookies are a hit with everyone who tries them. Full of chewy oats, sweet sliced dried apricots, golden sultanas and chunks of dark, bittersweet chocolatey goodness, you could almost pretend these are good for you … as long as you don't look too closely at the rest of the ingredients.

Makes 30–40 cookies

250 g butter, softened
¾ cup sugar
3 tbsp sweetened condensed milk
1 tsp vanilla extract
1¾ cups plain flour
¼ tsp salt
1 tsp baking powder

1½ cups rolled oats
200 g dark chocolate, chopped unevenly into chunks about a quarter the size of a square of chocolate
½ cup dried apricots, chopped into thirds or quarters
¾ cup sultanas

1 Preheat oven to 170°C. Line baking trays with baking paper.

2 Cream butter, sugar and condensed milk until very light and fluffy. This will take at least 5 minutes in a stand mixer, so allow 10 minutes if using a hand mixer. Beat in vanilla.

3 Add dry ingredients and mix well.

4 Add chocolate, apricots and sultanas and mix thoroughly. If you're not using a stand mixer, the best way to do this is to use your hands, as the mixture is very stiff.

5 Roll double tablespoon-sized scoops into balls (about 40 grams, if you are a perfectionist) and chill for at least 30 minutes. This step is very important; if the dough isn't chilled, the cookies will end up as flat as pancakes when you bake them.

6 Place chilled dough onto prepared trays, leaving about 5 cm of space around each cookie.

7 Bake for 15–20 minutes or until golden brown. If you're reusing your trays, make sure you cool them completely between batches or, again, you'll end up with pancakes.

8 Once cooked, leave cookies on the tray for a few minutes before sliding the baking paper with the cookies still attached onto a wire rack to cool completely. Once cold, store in an airtight container.

Baker's Note — Storing Leftover Sweetened Condensed Milk

Store any leftover condensed milk in the freezer. Leave it in the tin and cover well with plastic wrap. It will last about three months and you can use it directly from the freezer without defrosting. An added bonus is that frozen condensed milk is easier to scoop out with a heated measuring spoon than runny condensed milk.

Nanna Brown's *Shortbread*

This recipe was kindly given to me by a family friend (thanks, Doris!). It comes from her mother, Mrs Brown, who was well known about town for her delicious, buttery shortbread. I've discovered over the course of testing this recipe in a modern kitchen that the key to perfectly pale shortbread is to make sure you cook it in a non fan-forced oven (see Baker's Note below).

Makes about 30 pieces

225 g butter, softened
⅔ cup caster sugar
1 tsp vanilla extract
2⅔ cups plain flour

1   Preheat oven to 140°C. Line two baking trays with baking paper.

2   In a stand mixer, cream butter and sugar for 10 minutes. The sugar should have completely dissolved and you shouldn't feel any grains when you taste it. If you're doing this with a hand mixer, it may take up to 20 minutes, but it's the key to getting a buttery, smooth shortbread — so no shortcuts!

3   Beat in vanilla extract, then mix in flour until just combined.

4   Tip dough out onto a lightly floured work surface and form into a log about 5 cm in diameter. Use a sharp knife to cut 10 mm-thick rounds and place them cut-side down on the trays. Press gently with a (very clean!) meat tenderiser and compress biscuits to about 7 mm thick. Alternatively, cut rounds 7 mm thick and prick with a fork.

5   Bake for 40 minutes, rotating and turning trays after about 25 minutes. Biscuits are ready when they are only just starting to colour around the edges. Cool on wire racks.

Baker's Note — Fan-forced Versus Non Fan-forced Oven
All my recipes are developed and tested in a fan-forced oven, but this is one recipe where a non fan-forced oven produces a superior result. If your oven only does fan-forced, reduce the temperature to 120°C, rotate the baking sheets after 20 minutes and watch the biscuits very closely after the 30-minute mark to ensure they don't over-colour and become too crisp.

Variation
This is quite a sweet shortbread recipe as most old-fashioned recipes are. If you have perfected it and want to make it less sweet, try reducing the quantity of caster sugar by two tablespoons.

Spiced Ginger and Cardamom *Biscuits*

I love spicy biscuits and these are perfection, to my mind. They make great Christmas cookies (I make them every year and they're always a hit) and wonderful, tasty gingerbread men.

Makes 30–50 biscuits

70 g butter, softened
80 g brown sugar
3 tbsp blackstrap molasses
1 egg yolk
2 cups plain flour
½ tsp baking soda

2 tbsp ground cardamom
1 tbsp ground cinnamon
1 tbsp ground ginger
1 tsp ground nutmeg
2 tbsp milk

1   Cream butter and sugar until light and fluffy. Beat in molasses, then the egg yolk.

2   In another bowl, whisk together flour, baking soda and spices. Add to creamed mixture, along with the milk, and mix until a ball forms.

3   Tip onto the bench and knead briefly until smooth. Wrap in plastic wrap and chill for at least 30 minutes.

4   Preheat oven to 180°C. Line baking trays with baking paper.

5   Roll out dough to 3–4 mm thick and cut into desired shapes. Place on trays with a 2 cm gap between biscuits.

6   Bake for 12–14 minutes for gingerbread men and large shapes, and 10–12 minutes for bite-sized shapes. Biscuits are cooked when the edges start to colour slightly. Cool on a wire rack. Once cold, ice with royal icing (see Baker's Note below) and decorate with lollies, if desired.

Baker's Note — Royal Icing

Royal icing is the perfect way to finish off these cookies. Using an electric beater, beat together 1 egg white, 2 cups icing sugar and 1 tbsp lemon juice for about 5 minutes. It should be thick and very white. Spoon into a piping bag and decorate cold biscuits. Press lollies onto wet icing before it dries.

You can easily colour royal icing with either liquid or gel food colouring.

Royal icing will dry out very quickly so make sure you keep your bowl well covered with plastic wrap or a damp tea towel. It will also keep in the fridge for up to one week.

Lemon and Poppy Seed
Biscuits

These wonderfully crisp, lemony little biscuits studded with poppy seeds are perfect with a cuppa or even with a wee dram by the fireside after dinner.

Makes about 40 biscuits

2⅓ cups plain flour
½ tsp salt
½ cup icing sugar
⅓ cup caster sugar
zest of 2 lemons, finely grated

2 tbsp poppy seeds
180 g cold butter, cubed
1 egg
1 egg yolk

1   Place flour, salt, sugars, zest and poppy seeds in the bowl of a food processor and pulse briefly to combine.

2   Add butter and pulse until you get fine crumbs. Add egg and yolk and process again until the dough clumps.

3   Tip dough out onto a large piece of plastic wrap and squeeze together. Form into a log that is 7 cm in diameter and chill for at least 2 hours.

4   Preheat oven to 180°C. Line baking trays with baking paper.

5   Once dough is very firm use a sharp knife to slice it into rounds 5 mm thick and place directly on trays.

6   Bake for 10–12 minutes or until the biscuit edges just start to brown. Cool on a wire rack.

Baker's Note — Chilling Biscuit Dough

You'll find that many of my recipes call for biscuit dough to be chilled before it's shaped — just as for pastry. This allows the gluten to relax, and results in better-shaped biscuits when baked. If you don't chill the dough, your biscuits will often spread more than you want them to and you'll end up with overcooked little pancakes rather than nice crispy biscuits.

Banana and Yoghurt *Muffins*

This was one of the recipes I cooked for my School Certificate Home Economics exam almost 20 years ago, and it's still a favourite of mine. These muffins have great texture (light and fluffy, but slightly branny) and a lovely, just sweet enough, banana flavour. They got me an 'A' and I'm sure they'll do the same for you!

Makes 12 muffins

1¼ cups plain flour
1¼ cups wholemeal flour
1½ tsp baking powder
⅔ cup baking bran
⅔ cup raw sugar
125 g butter

2 tbsp golden syrup
⅓ cup milk
1 cup plain unsweetened yoghurt
1½ tsp baking soda
1 cup mashed banana

1   Preheat oven to 200°C. Grease a 12-hole muffin tin.

2   In a large bowl, whisk together flours, baking powder, bran and sugar.

3   In another bowl, melt butter and golden syrup (I microwave it for about 1 minute). Then stir in milk, yoghurt and baking soda.

4   Working quickly, pour liquid ingredients into dry, then add mashed banana and fold together.

5   Divide equally between muffin holes and allow to rest for 5 minutes.

6   Bake for 5 minutes, then reduce temperature to 180°C and bake for another 12–15 minutes.

7   Cool in tin for 5 minutes before turning out onto a wire rack to cool completely.

Baker's Note — Freezing
These muffins freeze exceptionally well. Wrap each one individually in plastic wrap and toss in the freezer. Perfect for lunch boxes or breakfasts on the run.

Ginger
Crunch

My version of this great Kiwi classic, is based on the recipe from that other Kiwi classic, the Edmonds Cookery Book, *but is a more gingery, crunchy version than the original.*

Makes about 24 squares

Base	Icing
180 g butter, softened	150 g butter
¾ cup sugar	1½ cups icing sugar
2¼ cups plain flour	¼ cup golden syrup
1 tbsp ground ginger	2 tbsp ground ginger
1½ tsp baking powder	1 tsp ground cardamom

1   Preheat oven to 190°C. Grease and line a 20 cm x 30 cm slice tin.

2   Cream butter and sugar until light and fluffy. Stir in remaining ingredients for the base until well combined.

3   Tip dough out onto the bench and knead briefly until it comes together in a ball. Press dough evenly into the base of the tin.

4   Bake for 20–25 minutes or until edges start to brown slightly.

5   While base is cooking, put all the icing ingredients into a medium-sized pot and cook over a medium heat, stirring constantly, until butter has melted and icing is smooth.

6   Pour the hot icing over the cooked base and set on a wire rack to cool. Once cold, remove from tin and cut into squares.

Variations
Add chopped nuts or crystallised ginger to the icing for an extra-crunchy ginger crunch. Or, for a chewier base, reduce the flour to 1½ cups and add ¾ cup rolled oats.

Sweet *Scones*

These deliciously light and fluffy scones are made with buttermilk instead of plain milk for extra lift and tenderness. If you've never tried buttermilk scones before, you'll be amazed at just how good they are. Serve with lashings of jam and cream for a lovely afternoon tea treat.

Makes 12 scones

4 cups plain flour
¼ cup caster sugar
4 tsp baking powder
90 g butter
2 cups buttermilk

whipped cream and raspberry jam
(see page 46), to serve

1   Preheat oven to 200°C. Line a baking tray with baking paper.

2   In a large bowl, whisk together flour, sugar and baking powder. Rub in butter with fingertips until you get a sandy consistency and the butter is no bigger than peas.

3   Add two-thirds of the buttermilk and stir quickly with a knife. Add more buttermilk and keep mixing until you get a very moist dough that sticks to your fingers in clumps.

4   Tip out onto bench and cut into 12 pieces. Place on tray about 3 cm apart.

5   Bake for 14–18 minutes or until well risen and golden brown. Cool on a wire rack.

Baker's Note — The Key to Perfect Scones

There are two things to keep in mind when making scones: work the dough as little as possible; and keep the mixture very moist.

To prevent overworking the dough, use a knife to mix the dough quickly. If you can, rather than shape it on the bench, tip it straight onto your baking sheet and cut the scones there.

The moisture content of the scones should be such that clumps of dough stick to your fingers when you touch it. I always feel that if you lose half a cup of the dough as you're shaping it (because it sticks to your fingers or the knife or the baking paper), then you've got the moisture right!

Variations

Date Scones: Add 2 tsp ground cinnamon and ½ cup (or more) chopped dates. The finely grated zest of a lemon is also a nice addition.

Pinwheels: Roll scone dough out to a 20 cm x 15 cm rectangle and brush with 50 g melted butter. Sprinkle over ½ cup brown sugar combined with 1 tbsp ground cinnamon. Roll dough up into a log and cut into 4 cm rounds.

Esme's Cheese and Herb *Scones*

Of all the delicious things that fellow Chelsea New Zealand's Hottest Home Baker *contestant Esme Dawson made on the show, her scones were the most impressive.*

Makes 8 large scones

3 cups plain flour
6 tsp baking powder
25 g butter, softened
375 g tasty cheese, grated

3 tbsp chopped fresh herbs (e.g. chives,
   parsley, rosemary)
600 ml buttermilk

1   Preheat oven to 220°C. Line a baking tray with baking paper.

2   Sift flour and baking powder into a large bowl. Rub in butter with your fingertips until you get a sandy consistency and the butter is no bigger than peas. Stir in cheese (reserve 1 cup) and herbs.

3   Add two-thirds of the buttermilk and stir quickly with a knife. Add more buttermilk and keep mixing until you get a very moist dough that sticks to your fingers in clumps.

4   Scrape the dough onto the prepared tray. Very carefully shape the dough into a rectangle about 24 cm x 12 cm (don't be too precise — the less you handle it the better).

5   Use a sharp knife to cut the dough into 8 pieces and carefully move them apart so there is about 2 cm of space between them. Sprinkle the reserved cheese evenly over top of scones.

6   Bake for 12–15 minutes or until golden brown.

Baker's Note — Buttermilk

If you have scone cravings but no buttermilk on hand, you can use soured milk as an acceptable substitute. Per cup of milk, add one tablespoon of lemon juice or vinegar. Stand at room temperature for at least 10 minutes. Stir well (lumps should have started to form) and use as per buttermilk.

You can also try as an alternative a 50/50 mix of milk and plain unsweetened yoghurt.

Variations

Add ham or cooked bacon to the dough. Try swapping some of the tasty cheese for another kind (e.g. feta). Add sliced sundried tomatoes.

Make Basic Cupcakes

There is nothing worse than a beautifully decorated cupcake that is dry and horrid when you bite into it. I've spent years perfecting my recipe so that I can whip up a batch of light, airy cupcakes in no time. Top with a simple buttercream (see page 36) and a few sprinkles and you have something to delight both young and old.

Makes 12 cupcakes

110 g butter, softened
½ cup caster sugar
¾ cup plain flour, plus 2 tbsp
2 tsp baking powder

¼ tsp salt
2 eggs
1 tsp vanilla extract

1   Preheat oven to 160°C. Line a 12-hole muffin tin with cupcake cases.

2   Place all ingredients in the bowl of a food processor or stand mixer and beat until light and fluffy. Scrape down the sides and beat again.

3   The batter should look light and airy, like
    mousse.

4   Two-thirds fill cupcake cases with batter
    (see Baker's Note below) .

5   Bake for 18–20 minutes or until cupcakes
    spring back when lightly touched. Cool
    in tin for 3 minutes before turning out
    onto a wire rack to cool completely. Ice
    and decorate once cold.

Baker's Note — Filling Cupcake Cases

To get the perfect balance of cupcake and icing you need to two-thirds fill the cases (unless the recipe specifically says otherwise). Sometimes this may mean you have a little batter left over or that you only get 10 or 11 cupcakes. It all depends on the exact size of your cases (they do vary) and how much air you beat into the batter. Too much batter and they will overflow, too little and you'll end up having to drown them in icing.

Variations

Here are some ways you can adapt this recipe:
- Remove 2 tbsp of flour from the measure and replace with 2 tbsp cocoa.
- Stir in ½ cup chocolate chips, raisins, lightly crushed berries or 100s and 1000s.
- Add lemon or other citrus zest, or flavoured essences.
- Add food colouring.

Cupcakes in
Ice cream Cones

These are super cute and a great alternative to messy ice cream at a kid's birthday party. Use small, flat-bottomed ice cream cones and make sure they don't have any holes in the bottom or your batter will run out!

Makes 24 cones

24 small, flat-bottomed ice cream cones
2 cups plain flour
2 cups sugar
2¼ tsp baking powder
¼ tsp salt
80 g butter, at room temperature

240 ml milk
2 eggs
2 tsp vanilla extract
1 recipe buttercream icing (see page 36)
100s and 1000s, to decorate

1   Preheat oven to 170°C. Get out two 12-hole muffin tins and stand ice cream cones in holes. If your cones are a bit wobbly, use your fingers to break off any protruding bits on the base.

2   Put flour, sugar, baking powder, salt and butter in the bowl of a stand mixer and mix on low speed until flour reaches a 'sandy' consistency.

3   Add half the milk and combine until just moistened.

4   In a small bowl, whisk together remaining milk, eggs and vanilla extract. Pour into flour mixture and mix on low until just combined. Scrape down sides and bottom of mixer, then increase speed to medium-low and mix for 2 minutes.

5   Spoon batter into a piping bag or jug and three-quarters fill each cone. If you only have room in your oven for one tray at a time, hold off filling the second lot of cones until you're ready to bake them (or they will go soggy).

6   Bake cones for 15–20 minutes or until cupcakes spring back when lightly touched. Cones will keep for about 24 hours in an airtight container before going soft.

7   Make the buttercream icing, then cover bowl with plastic wrap and place in fridge for about 30 minutes (or until firm enough to scoop).

8   Use an ice cream scoop to scoop out balls of buttercream and press onto the top of cupcakes. Press icing into a bowl of 100s and 1000s to finish.

Variation
If you have a favourite cupcake (or even cake) recipe, try baking it in ice cream cones. Pretty much any recipe will work as long as it bakes at a moderate-slow temperature (160–180°C) and takes no longer than about 20 minutes. If the temperature is too high or the baking time too long, the cones will burn.

Rainbow
Cupcakes

These brightly coloured little cupcakes are always a hit with children and are great fun to make with your kids to boot. Use gel colouring or a good dose of liquid colouring to get nice bright colours.

Makes 12 cupcakes

170 g butter, softened
170 g caster sugar
170 g plain flour
2½ tsp baking powder
¼ tsp salt

3 eggs
2 tsp vanilla extract
food colouring
1 recipe lemon buttercream icing (see page 36)
100s and 1000s, to decorate

1   Preheat oven to 160°C. Line a 12-hole muffin tin with cupcake cases.

2   Place butter, sugar, flour, baking powder, salt, eggs and vanilla in the bowl of a food processor or stand mixer and beat until light and fluffy. Scrape down the sides and beat again. The batter should look like mousse.

3   Divide batter evenly between six bowls and add food colouring to each bowl, mixing very well. Here I've used red, orange, yellow, green, blue and purple for rainbow colours.

4   Place a small (about 1 tsp) amount of the batter you want on the bottom of the cupcake (in this case purple) into the bottom of each cupcake case. Top with next colour (blue) and continue with remaining colours. The cases should be about three-quarters full — you may have some batter left over.

5   Bake for 15–20 minutes or until cupcakes spring back when lightly touched. Cool in tin for 3 minutes before turning out onto a wire rack to cool completely.

6   When cold, ice with a generous swirl of buttercream and sprinkle over 100s and 1000s to finish.

Variations
You can make these cupcakes in any combination of colours you like. Make camouflage cupcakes by using batters in shades of green and brown and top with chocolate icing. Try orange and black for Halloween or red and green for Christmas.

Coloured Cut-out *Biscuits*

These are my daughter's all-time favourite biscuits. Making them is a great way to get kids involved in the kitchen as they love to cut out the small shapes from the middle and swap the colours around. I always make them in four different colours (and freeze half the dough of each colour for next time).

Makes 20 or so biscuits of one colour

80 g butter, softened	food colouring
½ cup caster sugar	1⅔ cups plain flour
1 egg	½ tsp baking powder
1 tsp vanilla extract	¼ tsp salt

1. Cream butter and sugar until very pale and fluffy. Add egg and vanilla and beat well. Add food colouring and mix well (make it a couple of shades darker than you want, remembering that it will lighten up slightly when you add the flour).

2. Mix in flour, baking powder and salt until combined. Tip onto the bench and knead lightly until it forms a smooth ball.

3. Wrap in plastic wrap and chill for 1 hour. Repeat for each colour you want to make.

4. Preheat oven to 170°C and line baking trays with baking paper.

5. Roll out dough(s) to 4 mm thick and use a round cookie-cutter to cut out discs. Use small cookie-cutters to cut shapes from the centre of each biscuit, then swap the colours around. Gently press the shapes into the biscuits.

6. Bake for 8–12 minutes or until the edges just start to colour. Cool on a wire rack.

Baker's Note — Plain Biscuits

This dough is perfect for plain biscuits as they don't spread much and maintain their shape when baked. Double the mixture and cut out a variety of different shapes. When cool, ice with coloured royal icing (see Baker's Note on page 19).

Doughnut *Muffins*

You know those highly addictive little hot doughnuts you get from street vendors at markets and fairs? Well, these taste just like them. Enough said.

Makes 24 mini muffins

1¾ cups plain flour
1½ tsp baking powder
½ tsp salt
1 tsp ground nutmeg
1 tsp ground cinnamon
¼ cup oil (e.g. rice bran or canola)
¾ cup sugar

1 egg
½ cup milk

Topping
100 g butter
⅓ cup sugar
1 tbsp ground cinnamon

1   Preheat oven to 180°C. Grease two 12-hole mini muffin tins.

2   In a medium bowl, whisk together the flour, baking powder, salt, nutmeg and cinnamon.

3   In another medium bowl, whisk together the oil, sugar, egg and milk.

4   Fold the wet ingredients into the dry until just combined.

5   Three-quarters fill the muffin holes with batter. You will have some batter left over which you can bake in larger muffin tins, or use mini muffin tins again.

6   Bake for 10 minutes or until muffins spring back when lightly touched.

7   While muffins are cooking, prepare the topping. Melt butter in a small bowl and combine sugar and cinnamon in another small bowl.

8   When muffins are cooked, turn them out onto a wire rack. Dip each muffin into the melted butter then roll in the sugar mixture to coat well. Eat while still warm.

Baker's Note — Muffin Mixing

The key to light and fluffy muffins is to mix the dry and wet ingredients until only just combined. The first step is to make sure you whisk the dry ingredients together well in one bowl and the wet ingredients well in another bowl. That way, when you combine them you're mixing as little as possible.

Use a light hand, a large spoon and an 'under, over, then through' action.

Medici's
Friands

Much like the brownie, friands seem to be something that never live up to the hype when purchased from a café. Imagine my delight when I discovered the perfect friand at Café Medici, here in Martinborough. Crispy, chewy and soft all at once, this is the best friand recipe I've ever tried.

Makes 12 friands

5 egg whites
175 g butter, melted
1 cup ground almonds
1⅓ cups icing sugar
5 tbsp plain flour

⅓ cup desiccated coconut
¼ cup shredded coconut
jam (see page 46) or curd, to serve
icing sugar, to serve

1   Preheat oven to 180°C. Grease a 12-hole friand or muffin tin.

2   Whisk egg whites until foamy, then fold in butter, almonds, icing sugar, flour and desiccated coconut.

3   Spoon mixture into prepared holes, filling right to the top. Sprinkle each friand with a little shredded coconut.

4   Bake for 15–20 minutes or until friands are firm and the edges are crispy. Cool in tin for 5 minutes before turning out onto a wire rack to cool. When cool, top with a little jam or curd and dust with icing sugar to serve. Best eaten the day they're made.

Variations

You can make these wheat- and gluten-free by substituting the plain flour for fine rice flour.

If you prefer to top the friands with berries, you can use fresh or frozen. Just pop three berries on top of each friand before baking.

Raspberry and Oat *Muffins*

Oaty and full of tart raspberries, these muffins make a hearty morning tea or a great addition to the lunch box. They freeze well, if individually wrapped, so can also make a great breakfast on the run.

Makes 12 muffins

2 cups plain flour
1 cup rolled oats
2½ tsp baking powder
½ tsp salt
170 g butter, melted
1⅓ cups brown sugar

3 eggs
1½ tsp vanilla extract
2 cups frozen raspberries, lightly crushed with
 your fingers
raw sugar, for topping (optional)

1 Preheat oven to 180°C. Line a 12-hole muffin tin with muffin papers or cases.

2 In a large bowl, whisk together the flour, oats, baking powder and salt.

3 In a medium bowl, whisk together the butter, sugar, eggs and vanilla extract.

4 Add wet ingredients to dry and fold in with the raspberries until just combined.

5 Divide the batter between the muffin cases and sprinkle with raw sugar (if using).

6 Bake muffins for 18–20 minutes or until they spring back when lightly touched. Cool in the tin for 5 minutes, then remove and cool on a wire rack.

Baker's Note — Using Whole Frozen Berries
Make sure you gently crush frozen berries before they go into the batter (no need to defrost them). If you don't, the berries will either sink to the bottom or cause the muffins to collapse under their weight.

Make Homemade Jam

Homemade jam is a cinch to make using jam setting sugar, and it's also tastier and cheaper than bought jam. If you've never made jam before, then using jam setting sugar takes the guesswork out of it. Follow the method below and you'll have amazing jam in no time.

Makes 4–6 medium-sized jars

1 kg finely diced fruit (fresh, frozen, dried or canned)
1 kg Chelsea jam setting sugar
10 g butter

Before you start

1. Sterilise jars (see Baker's Note on page 47) and put two or three small saucers in the freezer to chill.

2. If using canned or thawed fruit, make sure you drain it very well before putting it in your pot because you do not need any extra liquid.

3. If using dried fruit, place it in a bowl and cover with boiling water. Leave to stand until it's plumped up to your liking. Drain well.

4. Use a food processor to finely chop fruit or slice it finely with a knife, then give it a bit of a mash. It needs to be fine because you only boil it with the sugar for 4 minutes and the fruit doesn't have as much time to break down as with traditional jam-making methods.

5. Resist adding extra water to your fruit when making jam. As the sugar dissolves it becomes very liquid so you don't need it — honest!

6. The ratio of 1 part sugar to 1 part fruit is *very* important. Do not try to 'stretch' your jam quantities by adding extra fruit. You can make less than the 1 kg that the pack suggests, but make sure you weigh your fruit beforehand. Don't try to make more than 1 kg as jams are best made in small quantities to maintain the flavours and consistency.

Method

1. Heat the fruit and sugar in a heavy-based pot over a low heat, stirring until sugar dissolves completely.

2   Once the jam is starting to simmer, stir in the butter (this helps to stop scum appearing on the surface of the jam), then increase the heat and bring to a rolling boil. A rolling boil is when you can run your spoon through the jam and the bubbles don't subside.

3   Boil for only 4 minutes before testing (time this!).

4   Test by putting a small spoonful onto a frozen saucer; let it sit for a moment to cool, then push your finger through it. If the surface starts to wrinkle or you can draw a clear line between two halves, it's set.

5   If your jam isn't set after 4 minutes, boil for another 1–2 minutes and test again. Sometimes the natural pectin levels of the fruit can cause this to happen.

6   Spoon or pour into sterilised jars, cover with lids and leave to cool.

Baker's Note — Sterilising Jars

I find the best way to sterilise jars and lids is to wash them, then put them still wet onto a tray and into a preheated 120°C oven. Leave them there until you need them (or for at least 20 minutes).

You can also use them piping hot from the dishwasher or put about 3 cm of water in the bottom of the jars and microwave on high for 1½–2 minutes (or until the water boils).

Whichever method you choose, make sure you handle sterilised jars with an oven mitt or very thick tea towel — they will be very hot! Oh, and always sterilise a couple of extra jars — just in case.

Great Aunty Joan's
Victoria Sponge

My great aunty Joan was well known for her light and airy sponge cake and I'm delighted to share the recipe with you. The key to perfect sponge cake is using very fresh eggs, and sifting the flour three times. If you have access to fresh duck eggs, they make an incredibly light sponge cake.

Serves 8–10

1 cup cornflour
1½ tsp baking powder
2 tsp plain flour
4 eggs, separated
2 tbsp boiling water

¾ cup caster sugar
1 tsp vanilla extract
raspberry jam (see page 46), whipped cream
    and strawberries, to serve

1   Preheat oven to 200°C. Line the base of two 23 cm cake tins with baking paper and grease and flour the sides. Do not line the sides as it makes for a sponge with sloped sides.

2   Sift together cornflour, baking powder and flour three times. This is important as it helps to aerate the sponge!

3   Beat eggs whites until stiff peaks form. Add boiling water and beat well again. Add sugar, a tablespoon at a time, beating continuously until sugar is dissolved. Add egg yolks and vanilla extract and beat well.

4   Carefully fold in sifted dry ingredients.

5   Divide batter equally between prepared tins (it's best to weigh rather than guess). Tap the tins gently on the bench to remove any large bubbles.

6   Bake for 20 minutes or until sponge springs back when lightly touched. Cool in tins for no more than 5 minutes before turning out onto a wire rack to cool completely.

7   Sandwich sponges together with raspberry jam and whipped cream. Top with more whipped cream and hulled strawberries, then serve.

Baker's Note — The 'Right-sized' Egg

I use size seven eggs (or large eggs) in all my baking, and the fresher the better. If you don't have size seven eggs to hand, use a size six (medium) or eight (jumbo) for most recipes (e.g. basic cake, cupcakes, loaves). Where eggs are one of the main ingredients (e.g. for a sponge or angel food cake or macarons), it's best to use size seven as the difference in liquid will affect the outcome of the recipe.

Triple Ginger Cake with *Lemon Glaze*

With three types of ginger — fresh, powdered and crystallised — this is a knock-your-socks-off, take-no-prisoners, not-for-the-ginger-dubious ginger cake. Dense and moist with a light lemon glaze that adds a lovely tang, it's one of my favourite cakes for pretty much any time of the day.

Serves 10–12

3 cups plain flour
2 tsp baking soda
1 tbsp ground cinnamon
1 tbsp ground ginger
1½ tsp ground cloves
¾ tsp salt
1½ cups brown sugar
1 cup vegetable oil (e.g. rice bran or canola)
½ cup treacle
½ cup blackstrap molasses

2 eggs
½ cup water
2 tbsp fresh ginger, minced
½ cup crystallised ginger, finely chopped

Lemon Glaze
3 cups icing sugar, sifted
1 tbsp lemon juice
¼ cup boiling water

1   Preheat oven to 170°C. Grease and flour an 8–10 cup capacity bundt or ring tin.

2   In a large bowl, whisk together flour, baking soda, spices and salt.

3   In another bowl, whisk together sugar, oil, treacle, molasses, eggs, water and fresh ginger.

4   Add liquid ingredients to the dry ingredients in three lots, stirring until just combined each time. Stir in crystallised ginger.

5   Pour batter into prepared tin.

6   Bake for 50–60 minutes or until a skewer inserted comes out with a few crumbs on it. Cool in tin for 30 minutes before turning out onto a rack to cool completely. Once cool, put cake in the fridge for 30 minutes.

7   While cake is in the fridge, make the lemon glaze by stirring together all ingredients until smooth. Transfer to a small jug.

8   Place cake on a wire rack over a piece of baking paper (to catch excess glaze). Pour still-hot glaze over cold cake. To get an even layer over the whole cake, you may need to use the excess that pools underneath the cake. Scrape it back into the jug and continue glazing cake.

Baker's Note — Bundt Tins

I baked this cake in a specially shaped bundt tin (sometimes called a Kugelhopf tin), but you could bake it in any 8–10 cup capacity ring tin. Bundt tins come in a wide variety of shapes (this cake was baked in a Nordic Ware Cathedral tin) and are available at good homeware and cooking stores.

Whole Orange *Cake*

This is a dense and moist cake that isn't too sweet so is great at any time of the day when you feel like a pick-me-up. The flavour increases as it ages so leaving it for a day or two, or even three, after baking produces the most flavoursome cake. It is lovely served slightly warm with a bit of thickened cream.

Serves 10–12

1 large orange (about 250 g), quartered with
   skin and pith left on
1½ cups raw sugar
200 g butter, softened

3 eggs
1½ cups plain flour
pinch of salt
icing sugar, for dusting

1   Preheat oven to 170°C. Grease and line a 20 cm round cake tin.

2   Place all ingredients except icing sugar in the bowl of a food processer and whizz until well combined.

3   Pour batter into prepared tin.

4   Bake for 50–60 minutes or until a skewer inserted in the middle comes out with a few crumbs on it. Cool in tin for 10 minutes before turning out onto a wire rack to cool completely. Once cold, dust lightly with sifted icing sugar.

Baker's Note — Perfect Oranges

Due to its simplicity, the key to this cake is a perfectly ripe and juicy orange, which is why it's best to slice it (and give it a wee taste test) before throwing it in the food processor.

If you can't get one large orange, replace it with two small oranges. Remove the pith and skin from one of them (and use only the flesh) or you will end up with a very bitter cake.

Rhubarb and Hazelnut *Tart*

This cake-like tart may seem like a lot of work but it really isn't once you get going. The flavours work incredibly well together and it's delicious served warm for afternoon tea or dessert with cream or ice cream.

Serves 6–8

Rhubarb
6–8 stalks rhubarb, trimmed and cut to
    width of tart tin
zest and juice of 1 orange
3 tbsp brown sugar

Tart
210 g hazelnuts, toasted (100 g finely ground,
    110 g chopped)
120 g butter, softened
⅔ cup brown sugar
zest of 1 orange, finely grated
1 egg
1 egg yolk

1 tsp vanilla extract
⅔ cup plain flour
2 tsp baking powder
1 tsp ground cinnamon

Topping
40 g butter
⅓ cup caster sugar
3 tbsp cream
1 tsp vanilla extract

icing sugar, to serve
zest of 1 orange, to serve

1   Preheat oven to 180°C. Grease a 35 cm x 12 cm loose-bottomed tart tin and set aside.

2   To roast the rhubarb, put rhubarb, orange zest and juice and brown sugar in a baking dish and cook until rhubarb starts to soften (10–15 minutes, depending on how thick the rhubarb is). Set aside to cool.

3   Pulse 100 g hazelnuts in a food processor until finely ground (nothing bigger than 2 mm). You need about 50 g for the tart (use the rest in the topping).

4   Cream butter, sugar and zest until light and fluffy. Add egg, yolk and vanilla extract and beat well. Fold in flour, baking powder, cinnamon and the 50 g ground hazelnuts.

5   Pour into prepared tart tin. Bake for 20 minutes or until the tart is set and firm to the touch.

6   While tart is cooking make the topping by cooking the butter and sugar over a low heat until it simmers and starts to colour. Stir in cream and vanilla extract until smooth. Mix in hazelnuts (both chopped and remaining ground).

7   Spoon hot topping over tart just from the oven (don't worry if the tart sinks in the middle, just fill it up with topping). Arrange roasted rhubarb over top and bake for another 10 minutes.

8   Cool in tin for 10 minutes before sliding onto a serving plate. Sprinkle lightly with sifted icing sugar and orange zest to serve.

Baker's Note — Toasting Nuts

Toasting brings out the flavour of the nuts. You can toast them on the stove top in a heavy-based frying pan or in the oven at 180°C. Either way, nuts are ready when you can smell them. Make sure you watch them closely as they cook as both methods can quickly result in burnt nuts which are unusable.

Variation

Any tart fruit would do well in this recipe. Try replacing the rhubarb with thickly sliced feijoas when they are in season and plentiful. The orange zest and juice can be replaced with lemon, and the hazelnuts with walnuts.

Traditional
Fruit Loaf

This recipe is one of my grandmother's and I have adored it since I was a child. Lightly spiced and full of plump fruit, it is delicious smothered in butter. The best thing about it is that the recipe makes two loaves, so you can eat one fresh and freeze the other. Just defrost on the bench overnight and you have deliciousness for morning tea without any hard work whatsoever. Genius.

Makes 2 loaves

450 g dried fruit (e.g. sultanas, raisins, currants, cranberries)

2 cups brown sugar, tightly packed

225 g butter

2 tbsp golden syrup

2 cups cold water

1 cup nuts (e.g. walnuts, pecans, almonds, Brazil), chopped

1 tsp vanilla extract

1½ tsp baking soda

4 cups plain flour

2 tsp baking powder

½ tsp salt

2 tsp ground ginger

2 tsp ground cinnamon

2 tsp ground mixed spice

1   Preheat oven to 180°C. Grease and line two 22 cm x 11 cm loaf tins, ensuring the baking paper comes up above the top edge of the tin by about 5 cm.

2   In a large saucepan (a soup or stock pot is best), place the dried fruit, sugar, butter, golden syrup, water and nuts and heat slowly until almost boiling.

3   Remove from heat. Add vanilla extract and baking soda, stirring well. Put aside to cool to lukewarm.

4   Sift dry ingredients into the largest bowl you own (it needs to be big!) and once fruit mixture has cooled stir it into the dry ingredients.

5   Spoon batter into prepared loaf tins, dividing it equally.

6   Bake for 50–60 minutes, rotating tins once at about the 35-minute mark. Loaves are cooked when a skewer inserted into the middle of the loaf comes out clean. Cool in tins until cold enough to touch, then turn out onto a wire rack to cool completely. Store in an airtight container or wrap well in a couple of layers of plastic wrap and freeze.

Variation
You can use any combination of dried fruit and nuts in this recipe so you can be as traditional (sultanas and walnuts) or exotic (cranberry, pineapple and almonds) as you want. You could even experiment by adding ½ cup dark or white chocolate chips into the dry ingredients to balance out all those healthy fruits and nuts.

Melt-and-mix
Banana Cake

This has to be the easiest, quickest and tastiest banana cake recipe ever. The addition of coffee essence may seem a little odd, but it really helps to bring out the banana flavour.

Makes one 23 cm square cake

200 g butter, melted
1 cup brown sugar
3 eggs
2 tsp vanilla extract
1 tbsp coffee essence
⅔ cup milk
2⅔ cups plain flour
2½ tsp baking powder
1½ tsp baking soda
4 medium bananas, mashed

Lemon and Passion Fruit Icing
3 cups icing sugar, sifted
4 tbsp passion fruit syrup or pulp
1 tbsp lemon juice
1 tbsp butter, softened
1 tbsp boiling water

1   Preheat oven to 180°C. Grease and line a 23 cm square tin.

2   In a medium bowl, whisk together butter, brown sugar, eggs, vanilla extract, coffee essence and milk.

3   In a large bowl, whisk together flour, baking powder and baking soda. Make a well in the middle and pour in the wet ingredients. Stir until almost combined, then add banana and stir until combined.

4   Spoon batter into prepared tin. Bake for 35–40 minutes or until a skewer inserted in the middle come out with just a few crumbs on it. Cool in tin for 10 minutes before turning out onto a wire rack to cool completely.

5   To make the icing, stir all ingredients together in a medium bowl until smooth. Add more icing sugar if you want it thicker. Spread icing over cold cake.

Baker's Note — Bananas
The riper the banana, the better for this cake as you'll get a stronger banana flavour. If you have bananas sitting around and they're past eating, freeze them until you feel the urge to bake. Simply defrost on the bench for about 20 minutes before peeling and mashing.

Variation — Chocolate Versus Lemon
The age-old debate about whether chocolate or lemon icing on banana cake is better is hotly contested in our house. I'm a lemon icing girl as I like the contrast in flavour, but chocolate icing is my husband's favourite. If you'd rather do chocolate icing, omit the passion fruit and lemon, increase the boiling water to 3 tablespoons and sift ¼ cup cocoa in with the icing sugar.

White
Cake

This is a great basic vanilla cake that is easy, tasty and can be coloured or flavoured in many ways, thanks to its 'whiteness'. Here, I've decorated it with Swiss meringue buttercream swirls (see page 146) but it's equally tasty with a good old-fashioned chocolate icing. For the Neapolitan Layer Cake (see page 188), I've coloured and flavoured half of the cake mixture to make the strawberry layer.

Makes two 23 cm round cakes

5 egg whites
¾ cup milk, at room temperature
4 tsp vanilla extract
2½ cups plain flour

1⅓ cups sugar
4 tsp baking powder
½ tsp salt
170 g butter, softened

1   Preheat oven to 180°C. Grease and line two 23 cm round tins.

2   In a small bowl, mix egg whites, ¼ cup milk and vanilla extract and set aside.

3   In the bowl of a stand mixer, blend the flour, sugar, baking powder and salt on a low speed for 30 seconds. Add the softened butter and the remaining milk. Increase the speed to medium and beat for 90 seconds. Scrape down the sides of the bowl well.

4   Add the egg whites in three lots, mixing on medium for 20 seconds after each addition and scraping down the bowl, too.

5   Divide the mixture between the tins (weigh them for accuracy).

6   Bake for 18–22 minutes or until a skewer inserted in the middle comes out clean. Cool the cakes in the tins for 10 minutes before turning out onto a wire rack to cool completely.

Baker's Note — Reverse Creaming Method
This way of making cakes is called the reverse creaming method and was pioneered by Rose Levy Beranbaum, doyenne of American baking. It's not a difficult method and it creates lovely light cakes, but it's important that you follow the instructions precisely. Firstly, make sure your butter is really soft, but not melted, or the flour won't mix in properly. Secondly, make sure you mix it for only the time specified or you will end up with a tough cake.

Banana, Fig and Honey *Loaf*

This dense, moist loaf is tasty, full of flavour and, without the addition of butter, is perfect for a healthy(ish) morning tea. It's best left to firm up a bit for a day before eating but, if you can't wait, it's just as delicious warm from the oven.

Makes 2 loaves

2 cups bran
200 g dried figs, chopped
1 cup wholemeal flour
1½ tsp baking powder
1 tsp baking soda
1 tsp ground cinnamon

1 tsp ground cardamom
¼ cup treacle
¼ cup runny honey
½ cup milk
¼ cup vegetable oil (e.g. rice bran or canola)
4 ripe bananas, mashed

1   Preheat oven to 180°C. Grease and line two 22 cm x 11 cm loaf tins.

2   Mix all ingredients together in a large bowl until combined.

3   Spoon batter into tins and spread out.

4   Bake for 30–40 minutes or until a skewer inserted comes out with a few crumbs on it.

5   Cool in tins on a wire rack for 15 minutes before turning out and cooling completely.

Baker's Note — Testing for 'Doneness'

When it comes to most dense cakes and loaves, the best way to test if they are done is to insert a skewer into the centre of the loaf or cake. When you pull it out it should still have a few crumbs attached to it. Many recipes state that the skewer should be free of crumbs when you remove it, but I prefer to have most things slightly 'underdone'. My reasoning (and experience) is that the cakes will continue to cook as they rest in the tins, and I'd rather have a moist cake than a dry one!

Spiced Apple *Squares*

Simple, tasty and easy to make, these squares are perfect served still warm from the oven for morning tea. I've made the recipe even easier by using tinned diced apple but if you'd prefer to do it from scratch, see the Baker's Note below for a quick and easy microwave method.

Makes one 23 cm square cake

75 g butter, softened
¾ cup brown sugar
1 egg
1 tsp vanilla extract
2 cups self-raising flour
2 tsp ground mixed spice

1 tsp ground cinnamon
⅓ cup milk
¾ cup walnuts, chopped
1 cup sultanas
1 x 380 g tin diced cooked apple
icing sugar, to serve

1   Preheat oven to 180°C. Grease and line a 23 cm square cake tin.

2   Cream butter and sugar until light and fluffy. Add egg and vanilla extract and beat well.

3   Mix in flour, mixed spice and cinnamon, then stir in milk. Fold in walnuts, sultanas and apple.

4   Spoon into prepared tin.

5   Bake for 30 minutes or until a skewer inserted in the middle comes out with just a few crumbs on it. Cool in tin for 10 minutes before turning out onto a wire rack. Once cool, cut into squares. Dust with icing sugar and serve.

Baker's Note — Microwaved Cooked Apple
Peel, core and dice apples, then place in a microwave-proof dish. Do not add water or sugar. Cover with a paper towel and cook on high for 3–4 minutes or until apple is soft (check after 2 minutes as microwaves vary in power). Cool to room temperature before using.

Great-grandma's
Fruit Cake

This recipe comes from my great-grandmother and has barely changed since she started making it over a century ago. It's a 'light' fruit cake (in colour, not weight!) and appeals to those who don't like a rich cake. It's perfect for weddings, special occasions and, of course, Christmas. Make it a month or two in advance to let the flavours really develop. Store well wrapped in plastic wrap then newspaper in a cool, dry, dark place.

Makes one large 23 cm square cake

1 kg mixed dried fruit

500 g other dried fruit and nuts (e.g. dates, prunes, apricots, almonds, Brazil nuts, hazelnuts)

4 cups plain flour

475 g butter, softened

2 cups sugar

10 eggs

2 tsp vanilla extract

½ tsp almond essence

zest of 1 lemon, finely grated

zest of 1 orange, finely grated

2 tbsp dark jam (e.g. blackcurrant, boysenberry or plum)

1 tsp baking powder

½ tsp salt

2 tsp milk

2 tsp golden syrup

70 g blanched almonds (optional)

brandy (I use about ⅓ cup), to taste (optional)

1   Preheat oven to 200°C. Line tin as per Baker's Note on page 67 (very important!).

2   Place dried fruits in a large bowl and sprinkle over 1 cup flour. Stir well to coat all the fruit and set aside (this stops the fruit from sinking to the bottom of the cake).

3   Cream butter and sugar until pale and fluffy. Add eggs, one at a time, beating well after each addition (the mixture will 'break' and looked curdled but don't worry about this).

4   Beat in vanilla extract, almond essence, zests and jam.

5   Fold in remaining flour, baking powder and salt. Mix until just combined.

6   Warm milk and golden syrup together and stir to combine. Add to batter with fruit. Stir well.

7   Spoon batter into prepared tin and spread evenly to the edges. Make a small, shallow, bowl-shaped hollow in the middle of the cake to allow for rising (if you don't, you will get a domed cake).

8   If using almonds, gently press into surface of cake in a decorative pattern.

9   Place in oven on top of four sheets of newspaper and immediately turn oven down to 130°C. Bake for 3–4 hours or until a skewer inserted in the middle comes out clean.

10   When cooked, remove from oven and sprinkle brandy liberally over hot cake. Cool in tin on a wire rack. When completely cool, either wrap securely and store or ice, as desired.

Baker's Note — Preparing Your Tin

This is one recipe where you need to spend time preparing your tin. Because the cake bakes for such a long period you need to make sure the outside doesn't dry out before the middle cooks.

Start by greasing your tin well, then line the base with baking paper. Line the sides of the tin with baking paper as well, making sure that the paper comes up about 10 cm above the top of the tin.

Take some newspaper and fold it so it's four sheets thick. Wrap it around the sides of the tin, lining up the top with the top of the baking paper and making sure that the sides are covered all the way to the base of the tin. Secure well (I find a stapler works best to hold it all together).

Fold or cut some more newspaper to be about 10 cm bigger all around than the base of the tin (again four sheets thick), and place the cake on this when it's in the oven.

Variation

This is a big stonking cake, designed to feed the masses. If you're baking for a smaller crowd, you could easily halve this recipe and bake it in a smaller tin. Prepare your tin in the same way and adjust cooking time accordingly.

Nanny's
Chocolate Cake

My grandmother is an amazing baker and this cake has been a firm favourite among her grandkids for years. It uses everyday store cupboard ingredients but is still moist, rich and bakes up to a nice high cake without drying out. It's great as a kid's birthday cake, as it can be 'carved' into whatever shape you need, and is just as wonderful warmed and served with a scoop of ice cream for dessert. Easily one of the best 'basic' chocolate cakes you'll ever come across.

Makes one large 23 cm round or square cake

170 g butter
¼ cup golden syrup
2 cups plain flour
⅔ cup cocoa
1 cup brown sugar
3 tsp baking powder
2 tsp baking soda

2 tsp instant coffee granules (the stronger, the better)
2 eggs
2 tsp vanilla extract
¼ tsp salt
1½ cups milk

1   Preheat oven to 170°C. Grease and line a 23 cm round or square tin.

2   Put butter and golden syrup in a small heatproof bowl and heat on high for 1 minute or until butter is melted. Stir until combined and set aside.

3   Place all the other ingredients in the bowl of a stand mixer and beat on medium-high for 5 minutes.

4   Scrape down sides of bowl, pour in butter and syrup and mix through.

5   Pour batter into prepared tin (it will be very runny).

6   Bake for 50–60 minutes or until a skewer inserted comes out with just a few crumbs on it.

7   Cool in tin for 10 minutes before turning out onto a wire rack to cool completely. This cake keeps really well in an airtight container.

Baker's Note — Shaped Tins

You can make this cake in pretty much any shaped tin you like. It's great for baking in shaped 'novelty' tins, as well as in the more common square, round or oblong. You can also bake it in a sheet cake tin; just adjust the baking time, as appropriate. It's also great baked as thinner layers, then assembled with icing (see page 188).

The Village Café's
Hummingbird Cake

The Village Café is located in the heart of Martinborough's main street. It's a popular hangout for locals during the week and overrun by visitors on the weekend. Chris and Bruce are renowned for their amazing range of delicious home-style baking and they have generously shared their recipe for the one item I can never resist — their amazing Hummingbird Cake.

Serves 10–12

375 g (about 3 large) bananas, mashed
½ cup passion fruit pulp
1 x 425 g tin crushed pineapple in juice
1⅓ cups sugar
1 cup vegetable oil (e.g. canola or rice bran)
3 eggs
½ tsp salt
1½ tsp ground cinnamon
1 tsp vanilla extract
3 cups plain flour
1¼ tsp baking soda

Cream Cheese Frosting
80 g cream cheese, softened
45 g butter, softened
3¼ cups icing sugar
1 tsp vanilla extract
1 tbsp lemon juice

passion fruit pulp, to decorate

1   Preheat oven to 180°C. Grease and line a 23 cm round cake tin.

2   Put all cake ingredients in a large bowl and mix until evenly combined.

3   Pour batter into prepared tin.

4   Bake for 1–1¼ hours or until a skewer inserted in the middle comes out with just a few crumbs on it.

5   Leave cake in tin and place on a wire rack to cool completely.

6   To make the frosting, beat cream cheese and butter until smooth. Add other ingredients and beat again until smooth. Spread generously over the top of cold cake and decorate with passion fruit pulp.

Variation
If you prefer a cake completely covered in frosting, increase the frosting ingredients by half and make as per instructions.

Mariangela's

Tiramisu

When I was eighteen I was lucky enough to be able to spend six months in Italy on a student exchange. One of my most enduring memories was watching my host mother, Mariangela, whip up her special tiramisu. As she is a doctor her version is much lighter and healthier than the traditional mascarpone and egg-based recipe — and much tastier for it!

Serves 6–8

1 x 200 g packet sponge finger biscuits (see
   Baker's Note below)
500 g cream cheese

½ cup icing sugar
2 cups of very strong coffee, cooled
cocoa, for dusting

1   Find a serving dish that is about 7–10 cm deep and layer the bottom with half a packet of sponge finger biscuits, leaving only very small gaps. Cut them to size if you have gaps that need filling.

2   Beat cream cheese and icing sugar until very light and fluffy. Add about ½ cup coffee and beat until smooth. Continue adding coffee and beating until you get the consistency of softly whipped cream (the amount of coffee you use will depend on its temperature).

3   Dribble some of the remaining coffee over the top of the sponge fingers. You want the top of the biscuits soaked but not the bottom — it normally takes about a tablespoon or so per biscuit.

4   Spread half the cream cheese mixture evenly over the biscuits and top with another layer of biscuits. Douse them with coffee again and top with the remaining cream cheese.

5   Sift over a generous layer of cocoa, cover with plastic wrap and refrigerate overnight. You can tell it's ready to eat when the cocoa has gone damp and dark, but the longer you leave it the better it will get.

Baker's Note — Sponge Finger, Lady Finger or Savoiardi Biscuits
These are Italian finger-shaped biscuits that can be found in most supermarkets. They are usually located in the international foods section, but sometimes they can be found shelved in the biscuit aisle or even with the gourmet food in and around deli sections. The packet size is fairly consistent across brands so don't worry if you don't have exactly 200 g.

Cheat's
Chocolate Trifle

By combining good-quality dark chocolate with ready-made custard you get an amazing dessert in a very short time frame. Perfect for those last-minute mid-week chocolate cravings.

Makes 4–6

1 x 225 g unfilled trifle sponge
250 g dark chocolate, chopped
1 x 600 ml carton ready-made custard
1 x 395 g tin dulce de leche (see Baker's Note on page 101)
¾ cup cream, whipped to medium peaks
chopped nuts, to serve

1   Break sponge cake into small pieces (about 4 cm x 4 cm) and set aside.

2   Melt chocolate in a small bowl in the microwave on a low heat in 30-second bursts (or in a bowl over simmering water). Stir into custard until well combined.

3   Place a generous spoonful of dulce de leche in the bottom of 4–6 single-serve jars, glasses or bowls. Scatter over pieces of trifle sponge, then pour over chocolate custard — you want the jar about half full. Use a knife to wriggle the sponge around so that it is covered in custard.

4   Add another spoonful of dulce de leche and repeat sponge and chocolate custard layers.

5   Top with a generous dollop of whipped cream. Heat a little dulche de leche in the microwave for 10 seconds at a time until it's runny, then drizzle over top of cream. Sprinkle with chopped nuts and serve.

Variation

If you want to make a more traditional trifle, leave out the chocolate and dulce de leche and use plain custard and a tin of peaches instead (and a splash of sherry, if you wish). Top with whipped cream and sliced strawberries and you have a quick and easy Christmas trifle.

Make Bread

There are few things more inviting and delicious than homemade bread fresh from the oven. Yes, it can be time-consuming and tough on the arms if you don't have a stand mixer to do all the hard work, but it's well worth the effort. Just be aware that most homemade bread is best eaten the day it is made as it doesn't contain preservatives like manufactured bread.

Note: I haven't included a recipe here as the ingredients for bread recipes differ. The method, however, remains the same. Follow the instructions in your recipe, using the notes below as guidance for what to look for at each stage.

Mixing and kneading with a stand mixer

1   Place all the dry ingredients (e.g. flour, yeast, salt, sugar, etc.) in the bowl of your stand mixer. Make a well in the centre and pour in liquid ingredients (e.g. water, milk, eggs, oil, etc.), reserving a small amount of the water or milk.

2   Attach the dough hook to your mixer and mix on low until all ingredients are combined.

3   At this point the dough should be very sticky and wet. Add more water if it's not, and mix again. The dough should stick to your fingers when touched and fall off the dough hook in a thick ribbon when it's raised up.

4   Increase the mixer speed to medium-low and knead until the dough is smooth, stretchy and satiny. You should be able to pull it away from the dough hook like a piece of elastic. This will take 5–10 minutes, depending on the type of dough and the amount you're making.

Mixing and kneading by hand

1   Place all the dry ingredients (e.g. flour, yeast, salt, sugar, etc.) in a large bowl. Make a well in the centre and pour in liquid ingredients (e.g. water, milk, eggs, oil, etc.), reserving a small amount of the water or milk.

2   Use a wooden spoon to combine the ingredients.

3   At this point the dough should be very sticky and wet. Add more water if it's not, and mix again. It should stick to your fingers when touched as well as sticking to the sides of the bowl.

4   Scrape the dough onto a lightly floured bench and gather it all up into a ball.

5   To knead, use the palm of your hand to push the far side of the dough away from you then fold it back on itself. Give it a quarter turn, then repeat.

6   When the dough is properly kneaded it should be smooth, stretchy and satiny. You should be able to stretch it like a piece of elastic. This will take 10–15 minutes, depending on the type of dough and the amount you're making.

Rising (or proving) and knocking back

1   Once your dough is kneaded, tip into a large lightly oiled bowl and cover with a tea towel.

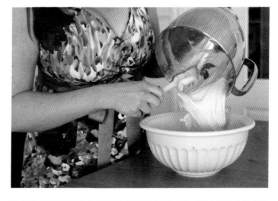

2   Place in a warm spot (see Baker's Note on page 78) to rise until doubled in size. Your recipe will indicate how long this normally takes, but it may be faster or slower depending on the room temperature.

3   When the dough has risen, knock it back by gently lifting the edges and folding it in on itself towards the middle. You don't want to knock all the air from the dough, just some of it, so gently is the key.

Shaping and final rise (or prove)

1   Shape the dough according to the recipe you're following and place it on the greased or lined tray, tin, etc. you are using to bake it.

2   Place the shaped dough in a warm spot to rise. You know it is ready to bake when you lightly press it with the tip of your finger and the indentation slowly springs back, leaving a small dent. If, when you press the dough, the indentation springs back quickly, it needs more proving time. If the indentation doesn't spring back at all, it's over-proved and you need to get it in the oven quickly (it will still taste great but won't rise as much in the baking process as it should).

3   Follow your recipe to finish and then bake your bread.

Baker's Note — Places to Rise (or Prove) Bread Dough

A hot-water cupboard or a very warm, sunny, still spot are the traditional places to rise (or prove) bread, but your oven is also a fantastic tool to use. Warm oven to about 50°C, then switch it off (very important!). Cover the bread dough with a tea towel and place in oven. Check the temperature every 30 minutes or so and turn the oven back on for a few minutes at a time to warm it back up. Set the timer when you turn it on so you don't forget to turn it off!

Wholemeal Bread Rolls
with Rosemary

I'm not usually a fan of wholemeal bread but these rolls are light, fluffy, soft and not at all reminiscent of the dry wholemeal bread of my childhood. I've made them in seasoned terracotta pots (see Baker's Note on page 81), but you could make them as regular rolls if you wish.

Makes 8 rolls

1 cup high grade flour	1¼ cups buttermilk, at room temperature
3 cups wholemeal flour	2 tbsp raw sugar
1½ tsp salt	4 tsp bread maker yeast
1 tbsp finely chopped fresh rosemary	130 g butter, cubed and softened
2 eggs	rosemary sprigs, to finish

1 In the bowl of a stand mixer (or a large bowl), combine flours, salt, rosemary, eggs, buttermilk, sugar and yeast. Stir well and leave to sit for 10 minutes.

2 With the mixer on low, add butter, one chunk at a time, mixing well.

3 Increase speed to medium-low and knead for 5 minutes or until dough is smooth and satiny (see page 76). It will still be a bit sticky.

4 Tip dough into a large oiled bowl and cover with a tea towel. Leave in a warm spot until doubled in size (about 2 hours).

5 Gently knock back, cover with plastic wrap and leave in the fridge overnight (or for at least 6 hours).

6 When you're ready to shape the dough, oil or butter well eight 9 cm tall, seasoned, clean terracotta pots and cover the hole in the bottom with a small piece of baking paper (or use a flattened mini cupcake case).

7 Tip dough out onto a lightly floured bench and divide into eight even-sized pieces (it's best to weigh them, if you can).

8 Form each piece of dough into a cone-like shape and drop 'point down' into the prepared terracotta pots. Leave in a warm place to rise for 1 hour. Preheat oven to 200°C.

9 When rolls are proved (i.e. dough springs back slowly when gently touched), use kitchen scissors to snip a small X on the tops.

10 Bake for 20–25 minutes or until well risen and brown on top.

11 When rolls are cooked, poke a small spring of rosemary in the middle of the X. Cool slightly and serve.

Baker's Note — Seasoning Terracotta Pots

It is very important to season your terracotta pots before you use them for the first time. To do this, preheat the oven to 190°C and give pots a good scrub in hot soapy water. Brush the inside and outside well with oil or butter and bake for 20–25 minutes. Repeat another two or three times — the more you do it, the more non-stick the surface will become. Cool before use.

Braided Blue Cheese and Walnut *Loaf*

This basic bread dough is perfect to turn into a variety of delicious flavoured breads. Here I've made two different-shaped and -flavoured breads to show you what can be done. Really the only limit is your imagination.

Makes 1 loaf and 8 rolls

Basic Bread Dough
4 cups high grade flour
2 tsp salt
4 tsp bread maker yeast
20 ml olive oil
340 ml water

Braided Blue Cheese and Walnut Loaf
⅓ cup toasted walnuts, chopped
100 g blue cheese

1   To make the bread dough combine flour, salt, yeast, oil and most of the water in a stand mixer or a large bowl. Mix until combined, add the rest of the water, if required, then knead until smooth and satiny (about 10 minutes).

2   Tip into an oiled bowl, cover with a clean tea towel and leave to rise in a warm place until double in size (about 2 hours).

3   Knock back gently, then divide into two equal parts.

4   Preheat oven to 190°C. Line two baking trays with baking paper.

Shaping the Braided Blue Cheese and Walnut Loaf

1   Roll one half of the dough out to a 40 cm x 25 cm rectangle and sprinkle with walnuts and blue cheese.

2   Roll dough firmly into a long sausage, then slice down the length of it to create two 'strands' which are still joined at the top end. Twist the two strands together, turning the dough so that the filling shows, and place on prepared baking tray to rise until doubled in size.

3   Bake braided loaf for 11–13 minutes, watching closely to ensure walnuts don't burn. Cool on a wire rack.

Feta, Sundried Tomato and Basil *Rolls*

basic bread dough
100 g crumbly feta, chopped
⅓ cup sundried tomatoes, finely sliced
½ cup basil leaves

Shaping the Feta, Sundried Tomato and Basil Rolls

1 Take the other half of the dough (see page 83) and roll out to a 35 cm square. Sprinkle top with feta, sundried tomatoes and basil. Roll up firmly along one side and use a sharp knife to cut into 8 equal-sized pieces.

2 Taking a piece of dough in both hands, push the inside up and out slightly so that the filling shows and place on prepared baking tray to rise until doubled in size.

3 Bake rolls for 11–13 minutes, watching closely to ensure sundried tomatoes don't burn. Cool on a wire rack.

Variations

Both the filling options and the shapes of these two types of bread can be endlessly changed. For an Asian-inspired twist try sweet chilli sauce and finely sliced precooked chicken. Or make good old-fashioned garlic bread by combining softened butter with roasted garlic and chopped parsley.

Spiral *Vege Tart*

It's amazing the difference presentation can make to a simple vegetable tart. By slicing the vegetables thinly and arranging them in a spiral pattern you can transform a dish from simple to sublime. To really make the dish sing, try it with my super-easy crispy cheese pastry. This is one dish where making your own pastry really makes a difference.

Serves 4–6

Cheese Pastry
150 g cold butter, diced
150 g tasty cheese, grated
1½ cups plain flour
¼ tsp salt
2 tsp ice-cold water

Filling
vegetables of your choice (e.g. carrots, courgettes, capsicum, pumpkin, field mushrooms, parsnip, eggplant)
2 eggs
¼ cup cream
salt and pepper
olive oil, to brush

1   Line the base of a 23 cm spring-form or fluted tart tin with baking paper and grease the sides well.

2   Make the pastry by combining butter, cheese, flour and salt in a food processor and pulsing until pastry comes together. You may need to add the water to make it clump into a ball. If so, add it a teaspoon at a time, pulsing after each addition.

3   Form pastry into a ball and flatten. Roll out to about 4 mm thick and use to line the tin. If using a spring-form tin, line to about 4 cm up the sides and trim the pastry. If using a shallow fluted tart tin, trim at the top of the tin.

4   Prick the pastry base all over with a fork and rest in the fridge for at least 30 minutes.

5   Preheat oven to 180°C, then prepare your veges. Using a vegetable peeler, mandolin or a very sharp knife, slice all the veges into long thin pieces. Try to make them no thicker than about 2 mm.

6   In a small bowl, lightly whisk together eggs, cream, salt and pepper. Pour into the base of your chilled tart tin.

7   Working quickly (so your pastry doesn't start to go soggy), arrange the vegetables in a spiral pattern, alternating veges on each 'ring'. I find it easier to start at the outside and work my way in. Once you've filled up the tin go back and poke leftover veges into any gaps. Brush the tart with olive oil. Bake for 30–40 minutes or until veges are soft and the egg is set.

8   Cool on a wire rack for 10 minutes before unmoulding and serving.

Baker's Note — Excess Pastry

This recipe deliberately makes more pastry than you need to line your tin, the reason being that the tart will look neater if you roll out a larger circle than required, then cut it to size (rather than trying to piece it together). You can freeze the leftover pastry or use it in smaller pies. It's also great baked off as crackers. Cut to desired size and bake on a lined tray at 180°C until crispy and starting to turn golden.

Variations

Extra cheesy: Add thinly sliced cheese in between some of the layers, or sprinkle feta on top of the cooked tart.
Meat-lovers: Add slices of bacon, ham or salami in between some of the vege layers.

Cheese
Crackers

These little cheese crackers take just a few minutes to make, use only six ingredients and pack a seriously cheesy punch. They are extremely addictive so if you're a cheese cracker fan, consider making a double batch or you may not have any left to serve friends and family!

Makes 40–50 crackers

1½ cups grated tasty cheese
60 g butter, softened
¾ cup plain flour
½ tsp salt

1 tsp smoked paprika (or ½ tsp strong Spanish paprika)
1 tbsp milk

1   Preheat oven to 170°C. Line two baking trays with baking paper.

2   Put everything except the milk in a food processor and pulse until you get coarse crumbs.

3   Add milk and pulse until it starts to come together in clumps.

4   Tip dough onto a lightly floured bench and press together with your hands to form a ball.

5   Roll out dough to about 3–4 mm thick and, using a sharp knife, cut into 5 cm squares.

6   Place squares on baking trays with about 1 cm space between them and press the end of a wooden spoon into the middle of each one to create a 'dimple' (this helps them cook more evenly).

7   Bake for 10–13 minutes or until just starting to turn brown around the edges.

8   Cool on a wire rack, try not to burn your mouth while testing them, and store in an airtight container.

Baker's Note — Cheese Type

Tasty cheese is a must for these crackers as anything else pales in comparison (I find the cheapest way to buy it is in house brand, pre-grated packets). However, if you have only mild or Colby in the fridge, then use 1 cup mild or Colby and ½ cup grated Parmesan to give the crackers a bit of punch.

Muffin Tin *Frittatas*

Delicious eaten hot from the oven for a weekend lunch, these individual frittatas also make great little lunch box treats. Wrap individually, freeze and pop into lunch boxes in the morning. They will be defrosted but still cool by lunchtime.

Makes 12 frittatas

8 eggs
½ cup cream
salt and pepper
½ cup grated cheese (tasty is best)
2 spring onions, finely chopped
½ cup sundried tomatoes, sliced

100 g feta, diced
100 g shaved ham, chopped
1 cup silver beet or spinach, chopped
2 tbsp finely chopped parsley

1   Preheat oven to 190°C. Thoroughly grease a 12-hole muffin tin.

2   In a large bowl, whisk together eggs, cream, salt and pepper until well combined.

3   Add all other ingredients and mix well.

4   Spoon mixture into prepared holes, filling right to the top.

5   Bake for 20 minutes or until puffed, golden and firm to the touch.

6   Cool on a wire rack for 5 minutes before removing from tin (frittatas will deflate while cooling so don't panic) to serve. If you're freezing them, cool to room temperature before sealing well in plastic wrap.

Variations
The variations on these are endless and only limited by your fridge stocks and your imagination:
Add extra cheese on top before baking — Parmesan is great.
Swap the ham for bacon, salmon, tinned tuna or salami.
Use whatever vegetables you have lying around in the vege bin (e.g. mushrooms, capsicums, courgettes).
Use cooled, diced roast veges or meat.

Decadent

Lashings of butter; dripping with chocolate; smothered in cream; coated in caramel. These are the things I picture when I imagine decadent treats for dessert, pudding and swish afternoon teas. Each of the recipes in this chapter is self-indulgent and sinful, but created with supermarket-sourced ingredients and straightforward techniques. Perfect for celebrating with (or showing off to) your friends and family, and well worth every calorie.

ARTISAN

500 ML

Make Macarons

Macarons have a reputation for being tricky little beasts to make and indeed they can be if you go into it with only a basic recipe to guide you. The key to spectacular macarons is knowing what you're looking for when you mix, pipe, rest and bake them. Follow the instructions below and the results are sure to impress even the fussiest macaron connoisseur.

Makes 20–30 paired and filled macarons

¾ cup ground almonds
1 cup icing sugar
2 egg whites
¼ cup caster sugar

1   Put almonds and icing sugar in a food processor and blend for about 30 seconds until the mixture is fine and powdery. Sift mixture into a bowl and discard any of the ground almonds that won't fit through the sieve. You can skip this step, but if you do you'll end up with grainy macarons.

2   Beat egg whites with an electric mixer until stiff peaks form. The peaks should stand firmly upright when you turn the beater upside down.

3   Gradually add in caster sugar, a
    tablespoon at a time. Beat well after each
    addition to make a firm, glossy meringue.
    It should look like shaving foam once all
    the sugar is dissolved.

4   Beat in colouring
    or liquid flavouring.

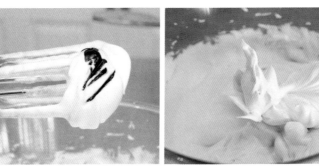

5   Add one-third of the almond mixture
    to the meringue. Using a spatula and a
    circular folding and cutting action, slowly
    fold in dry ingredients. Make sure you
    scrape the sides of the bowl as well. A
    light hand is best here!

6   Once all the almond mixture has been folded in, add the second third. As you fold in more dry
    ingredients the mixture will become firmer.

7   Add the final third of the almond mixture.
    Once it has all been incorporated the
    batter will be quite firm. Keep folding until
    the mixture starts to loosen. The final
    batter should be smooth and glossy and a
    thick ribbon of batter should fall from the
    spatula when you lift it up. If the batter
    falls off in a blob and not a ribbon, keep
    mixing!

8   Check the batter for the ribbon falling from the spatula every few turns to make sure you're not over-mixing. This step is very important: under-mixing will result in batter that is too firm and you will get mountainous macarons when you pipe them. Over-mixing will result in a batter that is too runny and will not hold a shape when you pipe.

9   Spoon mix into a piping bag fitted with a small round tip (or use a disposable bag and snip off the corner) and pipe 3–4 cm rounds on baking paper- or silicone-lined baking sheets. Ensure macrons are well spaced to allow for spreading. You can draw circles on the back of your baking paper as a guide (use a cookie cutter as a template) or go for the rustic, homemade look.

10 The best way to get a round, even macaron is to bury the tip of the piping bag in the batter as you pipe it out. If you squeeze with an even pressure, the batter will ooze out to form a circle.

11 Bang the baking sheet on the bench — quite hard! — to remove any air bubbles and use a damp finger to smooth down any bumps or peaks.

12 Leave to stand at room temperature for at least 30 minutes. Once set, you should be able to gently touch the macaron without any mixture sticking to your fingers. On humid or cold days, it will take longer for them to dry. This resting period creates the frilly foot that denotes a 'good' macaron so don't be tempted to cut the time short!

13 Preheat oven to 150°C or 160°C. The exact temperature and time will depend on your oven. Older, less efficient ovens should start at 160°C and newer, tight-sealing ovens at 150°C.

14 Bake the macarons *one* sheet at a time (very important!) for 10–15 minutes. Check after 6 minutes or so and if they're starting to brown, turn down the oven temperature by 10°C. The macarons are ready when they are firm on the top and the foot is starting to set.

15 Let the macarons cool on the baking sheet for 10 minutes (this continues cooking the base without drying them out), then slide the baking paper onto a wire rack to cool completely. Once cold, peel them off the paper, pair them up and fill them.

Baker's Note — Using Up Egg Yolks

Now you've made all those amazing macarons, what can you do with all the egg yolks you have left over?

They can be frozen (singly in ice-cube trays is best) for up to three months, then thawed in the fridge when you next need them.

Make a batch of curd (see page 164), leave out the passion fruit for lemon curd or add half a cup of another stewed fruit.

Substitute two egg yolks for one whole egg in your next cake or batch of biscuits … as long as the recipe doesn't specify the use of egg white, that is!

The Many Flavours of Macarons

One of the great things about the basic macaron recipe is that it is easily added to to create a range of flavoured macarons. By mastering the technique you'll have increased your recipe range immensely.

To the basic recipe add the following:

Lemon

- Add the zest of 1 lemon and a small amount of yellow food colouring to the meringue at the end of Step 4 and mix well. Fill cooked macarons with lemon curd. Note: other citrus flavours can be used, too.

Rosewater

- Add a few drops of pink food colouring and ½ tsp rosewater to the meringue at the end of Step 4 and mix well. Sprinkle with candied rose petals or dot on a wee bit of food colouring (use a toothpick) once you've piped the rounds (but before leaving them to set). Whip ⅔ cup cream with 2 tsp rosewater to make the filling.

Vanilla

- Add 1 tsp vanilla extract to meringue at the end of Step 4 and mix well. Fill with vanilla buttercream (see page 36).

Chocolate

- Remove 2 tbsp icing sugar from the icing sugar measure and add in 2 tbsp cocoa. Grind with almonds as usual. Fill with chocolate ganache (see page 124). Note: this substitution of 'flavour' for icing sugar works well with freeze-dried fruit powder, too.

Pistachio

- Replace ¼ cup ground almonds with ¼ cup ground pistachios and blend as usual with icing sugar. Add a few drops of green food colouring to the meringue at the end of Step 4 and mix well. Sprinkle 2 tbsp chopped pistachios over macarons once piped (but before they're set). Fill with buttercream (see page 36) coloured with green colouring and mixed with chopped pistachios. Note: this substitution of nuts works well. Try walnut filled with coffee buttercream (see page 36) as well.

Berry

- Colour meringue to suit fruit (e.g. pink for strawberry, blue for blueberry) at the end of Step 4 and mix well. Fill with buttercream (see page 36), or whipped cream mixed with crushed berries.

Shortbread with *Dulce de Leche*

'Dulce de leche' translates as 'sweet of milk' and has a wonderful smooth caramel flavour that will have you eating it from the tin with a spoon. It's so easy to make your own (see Baker's Note on page 101) and it tastes much better than the bought kind. These buttery vanilla shortbreads sandwiched together with dulce de leche are well worth the effort of mixing, chilling, rolling, chilling and baking.

Makes about 24 sandwiched shortbread

90 g butter, softened
½ cup caster sugar
1 cup plain flour
¾ cup cornflour
1 tsp baking powder
¼ tsp salt

1 egg
1 egg yolk
1 tsp vanilla extract
1 x 395 g tin dulce de leche
icing sugar, for dusting

1   Cream the butter and sugar until very light and fluffy.

2   Whisk together flour, cornflour, baking powder and salt in a small bowl and set aside.

3   Add the egg to the creamed butter and mix well. Add the egg yolk and vanilla and mix well.

4   Add dry ingredients and mix until it just comes together.

5   Tip dough out onto a large piece of plastic wrap and form it into a smooth ball. Flatten out, wrap in plastic wrap and refrigerate for at least 1 hour.

6   Preheat oven to 160°C. Line baking trays with baking paper.

7   Roll dough out on a well-floured surface until about 5 mm thick. The dough is very soft so make sure you rotate it between rolls to ensure it doesn't stick to the surface.

8   Using a round 5 cm cookie cutter, cut out biscuits and carefully transfer to the prepared baking trays. Chill again for 15–20 minutes or until the dough is very firm.

9   Bake for 8–10 minutes or until the shortbread just starts to colour around the edges. Cool on a wire rack.

10 Sandwich two biscuits together with a heaped teaspoonful of dulce de leche and sift a little icing sugar on top to finish.

Baker's Note — Crockpot Dulce de Leche

Put a tin (or three) of good-quality sweetened condensed milk in the bottom of your crockpot and cover completely with cold water (I can't stress enough that you cover it completely). Place the lid on the crockpot and cook on low for 8 hours (I usually put it on overnight). Remove tins from crockpot and cool on the bench before storing in the fridge.

As dulce de leche keeps forever in the fridge in the sealed tin, it makes sense to make two or three tins at once — assuming you can resist opening them and eating it by the spoonful, that is.

Sinfully Good Chocolate
Toffee Cookies

Not for the faint-hearted or weight loss-inclined, these cookies are dense, chewy and reminiscent of the best parts of a brownie. Studded with toffee, they make a delectably decadent afternoon tea or midnight snack. Try not to eat all the dough before you make it into cookies — it's worth the wait, believe me!

Makes about 45 cookies

½ cup plain flour
1 tsp baking powder
¼ tsp salt
450 g good dark chocolate (at least 60 per cent
    cocoa solids), chopped
70 g butter

450 g dark brown sugar
4 eggs
1 tbsp vanilla extract
250 g chocolate-covered hard toffees or
    caramels (e.g. Pixie Caramel, Rolo, etc.),
    roughly chopped

1   Whisk together flour, baking powder and salt in a small bowl and set aside.

2   Melt chocolate and butter in a bowl over a pot of simmering water. Alternatively, melt in the microwave on medium in 30-second bursts, stirring after each burst. Set aside to cool to lukewarm.

3   In the bowl of a stand mixer (or in a large bowl with an electric hand mixer), beat sugar and eggs until very thick and pale (about 5 minutes).

4   Pour chocolate mixture into egg mixture, add vanilla and beat well.

5   Fold in dry ingredients and then fold in toffee pieces.

6   The dough will be very runny and impossible to make cookies from in its current state so you must chill it for at least 45 minutes until stiff enough to form cookies. You can prepare up to this step and chill dough for up to 24 hours, if desired.

7   Preheat oven to 170°C. Line baking trays with baking paper.

8   Using an ice cream scoop or a tablespoon, place 2 tbsp amounts of dough on the trays, allowing room for them to spread. I find you get about eight on a 23 cm x 30 cm tray. Don't worry if your lumps of dough are not perfectly round. Push in any bits that are venturing off on their own, but don't stress about perfection.

9   Return unused dough to the fridge until you're ready to bake the next tray.

10 Bake one tray at a time for 10–15 minutes or until cookies start to crack on top but are still soft in the middle. Cool on trays for 5 minutes, then slide cookies still attached to baking paper onto wire racks to cool completely. Peel off baking paper once cold.

Baker's Note — Baking Trays

If you only have one or two baking trays and have multiple batches to bake, make sure you let the tray cool completely between batches. If you don't, the second and subsequent batches of cookies will spread more than the first (due to the latent heat in the tray) and you'll end up with pancakes, not cookies.

Raspberry and Chocolate *Tart*

This is one of those super-simple desserts that will wow people and make them think you're a genius baker. Don't tell them how easy it is, and bask in the praise.

Serves 8–10

250 g plain sweet biscuits
4 tbsp cocoa
110 g butter, melted

500 g good-quality dark chocolate, chopped
1¼ cups cream
1½ cups raspberries, fresh or frozen
extra cream and raspberries, to serve

1 Preheat oven to 170°C. Grease a 23–25 cm round, loose-bottomed tart tin.

2 Place biscuits in a food processor and whizz to a fine crumb. Add cocoa and whizz again to combine. Add melted butter and mix to combine.

3 Press evenly into the base and sides of the tin.

4 Bake for 15 minutes. Once cooked, set on a wire rack to cool.

5 In a microwave-safe bowl or a heavy-based saucepan, combine chocolate and cream and heat gently until melted and smooth.

6 Lightly crush the raspberries and spread evenly over the cooled base. Pour over chocolate and chill for at least 2 hours or until chocolate is set.

7 Remove tart from the fridge 10–15 minutes before serving and use a hot, dry knife to cut into wedges. Serve with lightly whipped cream and a few extra raspberries.

Baker's Note — Quality Chocolate

The higher the cocoa mass percentage, the better for this tart. I use Whittaker's 72 per cent Dark Ghana, which is perfect for this tart which has no added sugar. I would suggest 60 per cent as a minimum to get a great dark chocolatey hit. Check the ingredients list on the back of your chocolate pack to find out the cocoa mass percentage.

Chocolate Pecan Pie *Cheesecake*

This cheesecake combines two of the best desserts ever — baked cheesecake and pecan pie (with chocolate ganache for good measure) — and just screams decadence. It takes a while to make as it involves a few processes, but at least you're earning your calories!

Serves 10–12

Base
300 g sweet plain biscuits
140 g butter, melted
¼ cup brown sugar
2 tbsp cocoa

Pecan filling
50 g butter
¾ cup brown sugar
⅔ cup glucose syrup
140 g pecans
1 tsp vanilla extract
120 g 72 per cent dark chocolate, chopped

Cheesecake
500 g cream cheese, at room temperature
1 cup brown sugar
2 tbsp plain flour
3 eggs
½ cup cream
1 tsp vanilla extract

Ganache
125 g 72 per cent dark chocolate, chopped
⅓ cup cream

1 Preheat oven to 170°C. Line the base of a 23 cm round spring-form cake tin with baking paper and grease the sides thoroughly.

2 To make the base, pulse the biscuits in a food processor to a fine crumb. Add the butter, sugar and cocoa and process until combined.

3 Press the biscuit crumbs firmly into the base and sides of the tin. This may take a little time but it's worth the effort to get it well pressed and even.

4 Bake for 10 minutes, then cool in the tin on a wire rack.

5 Make the filling by melting the butter in a medium pan over a low heat. Stir in the sugar, glucose, pecans and vanilla and bring to a boil, stirring constantly.

6 Remove from heat and stir the chocolate through until it has all melted.

7 Pour onto cooked base, spread out evenly and set aside.

8 Reduce the oven temperature to 150°C and put a large roasting dish of water on the bottom rack of the oven.

9 To make the cheesecake, beat the cream cheese in the bowl of a stand mixer until light and fluffy.

10 Beat in the sugar and flour, then add the eggs, one at a time, beating well after each addition. Stir in the cream and vanilla extract.

11 Pour cheesecake mixture over filling. Place cheesecake tin in water bath in oven and bake for 1 hour. Turn the oven off, prop open the door with a rolled-up tea towel and leave tin in the oven for another 30 minutes. The cheesecake should still be a little wobbly in the middle.

12 Cool to room temperature, then chill in the fridge for at least 2 hours.

13 Make the ganache by heating the chocolate and cream in a microwave in short bursts, or in bowl over a pot of simmering water. Stir until combined, then spread evenly over chilled cheesecake and store, loosely covered, in fridge until needed.

14 To serve, unclip the spring-form tin and slip off base onto serving plate. Stand for 20 minutes before slicing with a large knife dipped in hot water.

Baker's Note — Glucose Syrup

You can find glucose syrup in the supermarket shelved with the sugar or golden syrup. It comes in a 500 g jar but keeps forever so don't worry about it going off. You could substitute it with light corn syrup, if that is more readily available.

Pomegranate Mousse
Squares

This is a lovely light mousse with an incredible texture. Pomegranate juice can be found with the veges in the vegetable chiller or with the fresh juices in your supermarket.

Makes 16 squares

Base
125 g sweet plain biscuits
2 tbsp cocoa
70 g butter, melted

Mousse
1¼ cups pomegranate juice, plus 3 tbsp
2½ tsp powdered gelatine

100 g white chocolate, chopped
2 cups cream, plus 2 tbsp
¼ cup caster sugar
pink food colouring
seeds of 1 pomegranate (see Baker's Note on
   page 109)

1   Line a 23 cm square high-sided cake tin with baking paper, making sure that the paper comes well above the sides so you can lift the square out.

2   To make the base, blend biscuits to a fine crumb in a food processor. Add cocoa and pulse to combine well. Add butter and pulse until combined. Press into the base of your lined tin and refrigerate until needed.

3   In a medium bowl, place 3 tbsp pomegranate juice with the gelatine and stir briskly with a fork to combine. Set aside.

4   In a small heatproof bowl, place chocolate and 2 tbsp cream. Heat on medium power in 15-second bursts, stirring well, until chocolate is melted and smooth. Alternatively, stir while heating over simmering water. Set aside to cool.

5   In a saucepan, combine remaining pomegranate juice and sugar and heat to just boiling. Pour over gelatine and whisk until dissolved.

6   Whip remaining cream with a few drops of food colouring until soft peaks form. Stir a few spoonfuls into the white chocolate mixture to loosen, then fold it all into the cream.

7   Pour pomegranate mixture into cream and whisk until smooth and combined.

8   Pour over chilled base and smooth top. Chill for at least 3 hours or preferably overnight.

9   Remove mousse from tin, top with pomegranate seeds, then use a sharp knife to slice into 16 squares.

Baker's Note — Deseeding Pomegranates

To remove the seeds from a pomegranate (without the juice staining the walls, floors and your clothes), use a small sharp knife to cut a circle out of the top of the fruit, then slice it into three or four pieces. Fill a bowl with water and place the fruit in it. With the fruit underwater, use your fingertips to scrape out the seeds. As the seeds separate from the husks they will sink and the husks will float. Use a small sieve to scoop out the floating husks and then strain the water and seeds though the sieve. Pick out any remaining husks and store seeds in a sealed container in the fridge.

Variation

You can swap the pomegranate juice for other fruit juice or even purée. Try raspberries, strawberries or even mangoes. To make a purée put the fruit through a blender, then strain through a sieve to remove any lumps or seeds.

Apple and Rhubarb Crème Brûlée *Cheesecake*

This is delicious any time of the year but I feel it really lends itself to the cooler autumn days when your mind turns to comforting and homely desserts. Layers of lightly spiced cooked apple and rhubarb pair beautifully with the creamy cheesecake and the crunchy brûlée topping. Brûlée torches can be found at all good kitchen stores and some hardware stores.

Serves 10–12

Base

180 g plain sweet biscuits
75 g butter, melted
3 apples, peeled, quartered and sliced thinly
4 stalks rhubarb, sliced into 2–3 cm chunks
1 tbsp lemon juice
50 g butter
2 tbsp sugar
90 ml cream
½ tsp ground nutmeg

Cheesecake

500 g cream cheese, at room temperature
1 cup caster sugar
2 tbsp plain flour
½ tsp ground ginger
½ tsp ground cinnamon
¼ tsp salt
3 eggs
½ cup cream
1 tbsp vanilla extract

Brûlée Topping

¼ cup icing sugar

1 Preheat oven to 160°C. Line the base of a 23 cm round spring-form cake tin with baking paper. Grease the sides of the tin well.

2 In a food processor, pulse biscuits to a fine crumb. Alternatively, place biscuits in a sealable plastic bag and crush with a rolling pin.

3 Combine biscuit crumbs and butter and mix well. Press evenly into the base of prepared tin.

4 Bake for 8–10 minutes or until the edges just start to change colour.

5 Cool on a wire rack, then wrap the outside of the tin in tin foil (see Baker's Note on page 111).

6 Combine apples, rhubarb and lemon juice in a small bowl.

7 Melt butter in a large pan over a medium heat. Stir in apples and rhubarb and cook for 2 minutes. Sprinkle with sugar and cook for a further 3 minutes, stirring regularly.

8 Add cream and nutmeg and lower heat. Stir continuously until cream is absorbed (about 10 minutes). Set aside to cool.

9 To make the cheesecake, beat cream cheese until smooth and fluffy. Add sugar, flour, ginger, cinnamon and salt and beat well. Add eggs and beat until smooth. Add cream and vanilla and mix well.

10 To assemble, spread apple and rhubarb over cooked biscuit base, then gently pour over cheesecake mix. Put the tin in a large roasting dish and place in the oven. Pour hot water into the roasting dish to about 4 cm up the sides of the cheesecake tin.

11 Bake for 70–80 minutes or until cheesecake has only a slight wobble.

12 Remove from water bath and place on a wire rack. Peel down tin foil to drain any water and leave to cool. Chill for at least 4 hours.

13 Once chilled, sprinkle the top evenly with icing sugar and, using a brûlée torch, carefully melt and caramelise the sugar on top of the cheesecake. Serve immediately.

Baker's Note — Preparing Cheesecake Tin for Water Baths

Some cheesecakes just cook better in a water bath. The key is to make it as watertight as possible using tin foil. However, unless you have the super-duper wide stuff, it won't reach across the bottom of your tin and up the sides far enough. The best thing to do is tear off two long sheets and place them back to back. Fold over one long edge a few times to make a nice flat, watertight seam, then wrap the tin foil up the sides of the tin. You can also use tape to make it extra watertight.

Tamarillo and Polenta
Upside-down Cake

Upside-down cake is a great way to show off fruit so make good use of tamarillos when they are in season with this deliciously different cake. The polenta adds a wonderful slightly chewy, slightly crunchy texture with a real bite.

Serves 8–10

Tamarillo Topping
50 g butter
½ cup brown sugar
7–8 tamarillos, peeled and each sliced into
    4 thick rounds

Cake
2 eggs
1 cup brown sugar
2 tsp vanilla extract
½ cup buttermilk
½ cup olive oil
¾ cup polenta
1 cup plain flour
2 tsp baking powder
½ tsp salt

1   Preheat oven to 170°C. Grease a 23 cm round spring-form cake tin and line the base with baking paper.

2   Melt butter and sugar together and spread over base of tin. Press tamarillo slices, cut-side down, into the butter and sugar mix. Arrange them so they touch and cover the whole base of the tin.

3   To make the cake, in a medium bowl whisk together eggs, sugar and vanilla extract.

4   Whisk in buttermilk and oil, then fold in polenta, flour, baking powder and salt.

5   Spoon batter over tamarillos and place tin in oven. To save having to scrub burnt sugar drips off the bottom of your oven, make sure you place an oven tray on the rack directly below the cake.

6   Bake for 50–60 minutes or until a skewer inserted in the middle comes out clean. Cool on a wire rack for 10 minutes before unclipping sides. Invert onto a serving plate and serve while still warm.

Baker's Note — Polenta

There are two types of polenta: quick cook and the original slow cook kind. I like to use the slow cook polenta as it gives a much firmer 'crunch'. You can find polenta in the supermarket shelved with either the rice and grains or the organic foods.

Variation

Swap the tamarillos for pineapple, pear, apple, quince or any other fruit you have to hand.

Make Pastry Cream (or Crème Pâtissière)

Pastry cream is to bakers as concrete is to builders — an essential part of their repertoire. This isn't a difficult recipe to master and the results are to die for, so give it a go.

Makes about 2 cups

7 egg yolks
¼ cup caster sugar
4 tbsp plain flour
4 tbsp cornflour

3 cups milk
1 tbsp vanilla extract
extra icing sugar, for dusting

1   In a large bowl, beat together the egg yolks and sugar until pale and fluffy. Fold in flour and cornflour and set aside.

2   In a heavy-based saucepan, combine milk and vanilla and bring to a boil over a low heat. Simmer for 2 minutes, then remove from heat and cool for 30 seconds.

3   Pour about ½ cup of the hot milk into the egg mixture and whisk vigorously until well combined. Slowly add the rest of the milk in a thin stream, whisking constantly. It is important to add milk to egg off the stove (not egg to milk on the stove) to prevent your eggs scrambling.

4   Return mixture to the pot and heat over a medium heat, whisking continuously, until it boils.

5   Boil for about 1 minute or until thick and smooth.

6   Pour pastry cream into a clean bowl and dust the top lightly with icing sugar to prevent a skin forming. Cool at room temperature, then store in the fridge.

Baker's Note — Crème Diplomat and Crème Anglaise

Crème diplomat is simply a lighter version of pastry cream and is great as a pie filling or to accompany a dessert. To make it, fold together an equal quantity of pastry cream and softly whipped cream.

Although not technically correct, if you have pastry cream on hand you can make a crème anglaise (or custard) that is a million times better than custard from powder. Whisk milk into pastry cream until you reach pouring consistency and reheat carefully in the microwave or on the stove top. Do not allow it to boil or it will thicken again.

Mango Tartlets with
Oaty Coconut Crust

These little tartlets look beautiful, have a wonderful balance of flavour and texture and are surprisingly easy to assemble. The tartlet shells are chewy and reminiscent of an Anzac biscuit, the pastry cream filling is sweet and velvety, and the mango adds a punch of sweet tropical bite. They would be a lovely end to either a dinner party or a casual barbecue.

Makes 6 tartlets

1½ cups rolled oats
⅔ cup shredded coconut
¼ cup brown sugar
¼ tsp salt

100 g butter, melted
3 cups pastry cream (see page 114)
2–3 ripe mangoes

1   Preheat oven to 170°C. Grease 6 small (10 cm) pie tins.

2   Pulse oats and coconut in a food processor until finely ground. Add sugar, salt and butter and pulse until just combined.

3   Divide base mixture evenly between pie tins and press firmly and evenly into base and sides.

4   Bake for 10–12 minutes or until tops start to brown slightly. Leave bases in tins and cool on a wire rack. Bases can be made up to 48 hours beforehand and stored in an airtight container until required.

5   Peel the skin off the mangoes and slice lengthways down the side of the stones to get two 'cheeks'. Slice the cheeks widthways into about 3 mm slices and set aside.

6   Once tartlet cases are cool, fill with approximately ½ cup pastry cream each and smooth the top as much as possible.

7   Starting in the middle with your smallest slice of mango, curl the mango into a tight curl and place in the centre of the cream. It may refuse to stay curled up, but don't worry — simply hold it in position and continue placing slices of mango around the centre, layering them like rose petals, until you reach the outside edge. Fill in any gaps with leftover mango petals so you don't have any pastry cream showing.

8   They are best enjoyed as soon as they are assembled but can be stored for 1–2 hours in the fridge, if required.

Baker's Note — How to Tell if a Mango is Ripe

There are few things as horrid as an unripe mango so make sure yours is perfectly ripe before making this dessert. Colour is not an indicator of ripeness. Instead, press gently on the skin and if it gives a little, it is ready to eat. Unripe mangoes should be stored at room temperature until ripe, then stored in the fridge where they will last about five days.

Variations

You can replace the fruit with pretty much any other in-season fruit. Peaches, apples and pears can all be arranged in the same rose shape as mangoes. To stop the edges of these fruits turning brown, dip them in a bowl of cold water mixed with a bit of lemon juice.

Sticky Date Puddings with

Butterscotch Sauce

This recipe was given to me by my sister-in-law (thanks, Mel!) and it is my favourite sticky date pudding recipe by miles — spicy and flavoursome and a breeze to whip up. Oh, and the butterscotch sauce is irresistible. Serve with a scoop of good-quality vanilla ice cream.

Makes 4 small puddings

Puddings
185 g dried dates, chopped
1 tsp baking soda
½ cup boiling water
130 g butter, softened
1 cup brown sugar
1 egg
1½ cups plain flour
1 tsp ground ginger

1 tsp ground mixed spice
½ tsp salt
1 apple, peeled, cored and diced
½ cup crystallised ginger, chopped

Butterscotch Sauce
75 g butter
¾ cup brown sugar
¾ cup cream

1   Preheat oven to 160°C. Line the bases of four 10 cm round cake tins and grease the sides really well.

2   Put the dates, baking soda and boiling water into a small bowl. Stir well and set aside.

3   Cream butter and sugar until light and fluffy. Add egg and beat well.

4   Fold in flour, ground ginger, mixed spice and salt, as well as the dates.

5   Stir through apple and crystallised ginger.

6   Divide batter evenly among prepared tins.

7   Bake for 25–30 minutes or until a skewer inserted comes out with just a few crumbs on it. Cool on a wire rack.

8   While cakes are cooking, make the butterscotch sauce. Place all ingredients in a small pot over a medium heat and stir until it reaches a boil. Boil for 5–8 minutes, stirring occasionally until thickened.

9   Serve cakes warm with a scoop of vanilla ice cream and a generous measure of butterscotch sauce.

Baker's Note — Butterscotch Sauce
This sauce will keep for 2–3 weeks in an airtight container in the fridge. Just reheat portions in the microwave, as required. A good pinch of coarse salt adds a distinctly different note when it's served with ice cream.

Variation
Cook as one large cake in a 20 cm round cake tin for 40 minutes.

Little Kumara Cakes with Maple Cream Cheese *Frosting*

These lovely little cakes are beautifully spiced, moist and delicious. They're topped with maple cream cheese frosting and a pool of maple syrup, which makes them a decadent end to a meal or a lovely addition to an afternoon tea.

Makes 10 cakes

1¼ cups brown sugar
¾ cup vegetable oil
3 eggs
1½ cups plain flour
1½ tsp baking powder
1 tsp baking soda
3 tsp ground ginger
3 tsp ground cinnamon
1 tsp ground cardamom
½ tsp salt

2½ cups grated kumara, firmly packed
70 g walnuts, chopped
⅔ cup sultanas or raisins

Maple Cream Cheese Frosting
250 g cream cheese, at room temperature
125 g butter, softened
2 tbsp maple syrup, plus extra to decorate
½ tsp vanilla extract
2½ cups icing sugar

1   Preheat oven to 180°C. Grease 10 holes of two large 6-hole muffin tins.

2   Put the sugar and oil in the bowl of a stand mixer and beat for 3 minutes on medium. Add eggs, one at a time, beating well after each addition.

3   In another bowl, whisk together flour, baking powder, baking soda, ginger, cinnamon, cardamom and salt. Fold into wet ingredients, then fold in kumara, walnuts and sultanas.

4   Three-quarters fill the 10 holes in the prepared tins.

5   Bake for 20–25 minutes or until a skewer inserted comes out with a few crumbs on it. Cool in tins for 5 minutes, then turn out onto a wire rack to cool completely.

6   To make the frosting, beat the cream cheese and butter in the bowl of a stand mixer until light and fluffy (at least 5 minutes). Add maple syrup and vanilla and beat again. Add the icing sugar and beat until light and fluffy.

7   Spoon the frosting onto the cooled cakes, using a knife to smooth the sides and a teaspoon to make a small hollow in the top. Fill the hollow with maple syrup and serve.

Baker's Note — Making in Advance

These little cakes are great 'keepers' so are perfect to make in advance. Store them in an airtight container and ice when required. The frosting will also keep well in the fridge in an airtight container. Bring the required quantity back to room temperature and beat briefly to return to a fluffy texture before icing the cakes.

HOW TO

Make Choux Pastry

Choux pastry has a reputation for being difficult to master, but it's really all about technique. If you follow the instructions to the letter and don't open the oven until they're done, you'll end up with light, puffy choux pastry that won't disappoint.

Makes about 30 choux buns

125 ml milk
125 ml water
100 g butter, diced
½ tsp salt

1 tsp caster sugar
1¼ cups plain flour
5 eggs

1   In a medium saucepan, combine milk, water, butter, salt and sugar and bring to a boil over a low heat. When it boils, immediately remove from the heat and sprinkle the flour over. Mix with a wooden spoon until completely smooth.

2   Return saucepan to a medium heat and stir continuously for about 1 minute (this dries out the mixture).

3   Tip mixture into a bowl and leave to cool for about 5 minutes or until it is no longer too hot to touch (this ensures you don't cook the eggs when you add them).

4   Add the eggs, one at a time, beating well with a wooden spoon after each addition.

5 Once all the eggs are beaten in, the batter should be smooth, shiny and fall from your spoon in a thick ribbon.

6 Preheat oven to 200°C. Line baking trays with baking paper. Fill a piping bag with the batter, cut a corner so you have a 1 cm tip (or use an icing tip) and pipe 3 cm rounds, well spaced, on the baking tray (I normally get about 12 per baking tray).

7 Immediately put the tray in the oven (one tray at a time). Bake for 15 minutes at 200°C, then lower the heat to 180°C and bake for a further 15 minutes until golden, crisp and dry.

8 Once cooked, transfer buns from the tray to a wire rack to cool (use a knife or a small spatula so you don't squash them!).

NOTE: Choux pastry puffs up because of the steam created by the eggs. For this reason you must bake trays one at a time. If you are using the same oven for each batch, make sure you turn it back up to 200°C before putting the next batch in and only pipe each batch once the previous one is out of the oven.

Variation
To make savoury choux pastry, omit the sugar and add ½ tsp paprika or a pinch of cayenne pepper. Fill with salmon or mushroom mousse, or a thick cheese sauce.

Profiteroles with
Chocolate Pastry Cream

These are heaven on earth. Crisp choux pastry shells, amazing creamy chocolate custard and rich chocolate ganache make them my favourite French pastry.

Makes about 30 profiteroles

1 recipe choux pastry (see page 122)
1 recipe pastry cream (see page 114)
150 g dark chocolate, chopped

Ganache
250 g dark chocolate, chopped
½ cup cream

1 Make choux buns (see page 122) and set aside to cool.

2 Make pastry cream (see page 114) and stir in chopped chocolate at the end of Step 5 (i.e. once cooked but still in the pot). Stir until chocolate is melted and smooth. Set aside to cool.

3 Make ganache by heating the chocolate and cream in a microwave in short bursts or in bowl over a pot of simmering water.

4 To assemble, place a 3 mm round piping tip in the bottom of a disposable piping bag and fill with pastry cream. Use the piping tip to poke a small hole in the bottom of each choux bun then fill with pastry cream. Top with ganache and serve.

Variations
Simple cream puffs can be made by filling choux buns with sweetened whipped cream and dusting the tops with icing sugar.

Éclairs
Make chocolate éclairs by piping strips of choux pastry 10 cm long with a wide piping tip and baking as per the recipe. Fill with chocolate pastry cream and top with ganache, or fill with plain whipped cream and top with chocolate icing. Makes 20 éclairs.

Chocolate and Toffee
Cupcakes

There's something about a hedonistic chocolate cupcake that makes it very hard to walk past. Add a light and fluffy caramel frosting, chopped chocolate-covered hard toffee, and you have the perfect chocoholic's indulgence.

Makes 12 cupcakes

1 cup plain flour	**Caramel Frosting**
1 cup brown sugar	125 g butter
⅓ cup cocoa	1 cup brown sugar
½ tsp baking soda	⅓ cup cream
125 g butter, melted and still warm	¼ tsp salt
2 eggs	2–3 cups icing sugar
1 tsp vanilla extract	
½ cup strong coffee, still hot	chocolate-covered hard toffees or caramels (e.g. Pixie Caramel, Rollo, etc.), chopped
	1 tsp rock salt (optional)

1　Preheat oven to 170°C. Line a 12-hole muffin tin with cupcake cases.

2　In the bowl of a stand mixer (or a large bowl), combine flour, sugar, cocoa and baking soda.

3　In another bowl, whisk together butter, eggs and vanilla.

4　Add egg mixture to the dry ingredients and beat on medium for 20 seconds (or beat well with a wooden spoon for 1 minute). Pour in hot coffee and beat for another 20 seconds or until smooth.

5　Two-thirds fill cupcake cases. Bake for 18–20 minutes or until cupcakes spring back when lightly touched.

6　Cool cupcakes in tin for 3 minutes before turning out onto a wire rack to cool completely.

7　To make frosting, melt butter in a medium saucepan. Add brown sugar and cream and stir over a medium heat until sugar is dissolved. Stir in salt.

8　Simmer for 1 minute, then put aside to cool to room temperature.

9　Add 2 cups icing sugar and beat until smooth. Keep adding icing sugar in ¼ cup increments until you get a stiff piping (or slathering) consistency.

10　Pipe or slather tops of cold cupcakes with frosting and press the sides into chopped toffee. Sprinkle the tops with a pinch of rock salt, if desired.

Variations
This is a great rich basic chocolate cupcake that can be topped with pretty much any combination of frosting and chopped confectionary. Try lime frosting with chopped chocolate coconut lollies. Or vanilla frosting with jelly beans, Pebbles or Pineapple Lumps.

Tequila and Lime
Cupcakes

Like many former university students, I have good, bad and slightly fuzzy memories of tequila and lime. Thankfully, these lovely light little cupcakes only bring back the good ones! But be warned, the frosting packs a punch.

Makes 12 cupcakes

1 cup plain flour
1 tsp baking powder
¼ tsp salt
85 g butter, softened
⅔ cup sugar
2 eggs
zest and juice of 2 limes
¼ tsp vanilla extract
2 tbsp tequila, plus 2 tbsp to brush cupcakes
¼ cup milk

Tequila and Lime Frosting
250 g butter
2¾ cups icing sugar
1 tbsp lime juice
zest of 1 lime, finely grated
2 tbsp tequila

rock salt and lime zest, to decorate

1   Preheat oven to 165°C. Line a 12-hole muffin tin with cupcake cases.

2   In a small bowl, whisk together flour, baking powder and salt.

3   Cream butter and sugar until light and fluffy. Add eggs, one at a time, beating well after each addition. Beat in zest, juice, vanilla extract and tequila.

4   Add half the dry ingredients and stir to combine. Add the milk and stir to combine. Add the remaining dry ingredients and combine.

5   Spoon mixture into cupcake cases and bake for 20–25 minutes or until cupcakes spring back when lightly touched. Once cooked, remove from oven and immediately brush the tops of the cupcakes with the extra tequila. Cool on a wire rack.

6   To make the frosting, beat the butter until light and fluffy. Add the other ingredients and beat until fluffy again.

7   Pipe or spoon icing onto completely cold cupcakes and top with a pinch of rock salt and a wee sprinkle of lime zest.

Baker's Note — R18 Cupcakes
As the tequila that is brushed on the cupcakes and the tequila in the frosting isn't cooked off, it does retain its alcoholic properties. Therefore it's best to restrict the consumption of these cupcakes to those old enough to handle them.

Coconut, Pineapple and *Lime Cupcakes*

These tropics-inspired cupcakes look incredible and taste great, and require very little effort on your part. The pineapple flowers are very easy to make and make even the most humble little cake look like a million dollars.

Makes 12 cupcakes

1 cup plain flour
⅔ cup caster sugar
1½ tsp baking powder
¼ tsp salt
40 g butter, softened
zest of 2 limes
½ cup coconut cream
½ tsp vanilla extract
1 egg
1 x 227 g tin crushed pineapple, well drained

Coconut Frosting

2½ cups icing sugar
120 g butter, softened
¼ cup coconut cream

1 cup shaved or shredded coconut, or pineapple flowers (see Baker's Note below)

1   Preheat oven to 170°C. Line a 12-hole muffin tin with cupcake cases.

2   Mix together flour, sugar, baking powder, salt and butter in a stand mixer on low until it looks like sand.

3   Add zest, coconut cream and vanilla and mix well. Add egg and mix well.

4   One-third fill cupcake cases, then place a teaspoon of pineapple on top of batter. Fill cases to two-thirds full with remaining batter.

5   Bake for 20–25 minutes or until golden brown and cupcakes spring back when lightly touched. Remove from tin and cool on a wire rack.

6   While cupcakes are cooling, make the frosting. In the bowl of a stand mixer or food processor on medium-low, mix together the sugar and butter until combined. Add coconut cream and increase speed to high. Beat for at least 5–10 minutes or until frosting is light, fluffy and white in colour.

7   Ice cupcakes when cool by spreading or piping on frosting and topping with a small handful of coconut or a pineapple flower.

Baker's Note — Pineapple Flowers

Preheat oven to 100°C. Remove the skin of a not-quite-ripe pineapple. Use a small knife to remove all the 'eyes' and seeds. Slice the pineapple as thinly as you can (almost see-through is best) and lay the slices in a single layer on a baking tray. Bake until pineapple is golden brown on the edges and dehydrated, turning the slices every 40 minutes. How long it takes will depend on how thinly you sliced the pineapple and how juicy it is (it can take up to 3 hours). Once they are cooked to your liking, place them in a muffin tin to cool and form the flower shape.

Providore's
Turtle Slice

Providore Food and Catering is well frequented by Martinborough locals in need of lunch or a delicious quick dinner. With just a small shop front and only a few tables, it caters mainly for takeaway food (the sandwiches, frittatas and ready-to-eat meals are incredible) and does a roaring trade in catering for events and weddings. Their turtle slice is an indulgent piece of heaven and is a firm favourite of many, including the local constable.

Makes about 32 pieces

250 g plain sweet biscuits
125 g butter, melted
300 g dark chocolate, chopped
¾ cup raisins

¾ cup dried apricots, sliced
1½ cups desiccated coconut
140 g slivered almonds
2 x 395 g tins sweetened condensed milk

1 Preheat oven to 180°C. Grease and line a high-sided 22 cm x 32 cm baking tin (I use a roasting dish).

2 In a food processor, pulse biscuits to a fine crumb. Alternatively, place biscuits in a sealable plastic bag and crush with a rolling pin.

3 Combine biscuit crumbs and butter and press into the base of the tin.

4 In a medium bowl, combine chocolate, raisins, apricots and coconut and mix well. Spread evenly over base.

5 Sprinkle almonds evenly all over chocolate mix and pour condensed milk over that.

6 Bake for 30 minutes or until almonds are golden brown. Cool in tin on a wire rack before turning out and slicing with a large sharp knife.

Baker's Note — Sweetened Condensed Milk
Sweetened condensed milk is one ingredient where I always buy the best quality. For some reason house brands are never as thick and delicious as the branded condensed milk, and it really does affect the result.

Peanut Butter and Caramel Slice
with Salted Chocolate

If I ever want something rich, delicious and incredibly decadent, this is what I make. The addition of peanut butter and salt makes this a very grown-up version of a childhood classic. I use a high-sided 17 cm x 27 cm slice tray to make this in as I like a really thick layer of caramel. If you'd prefer a thinner layer, use a larger slice tin. Make sure you use good-quality sweetened condensed milk for this recipe, too.

Makes 24–36 pieces

1 cup plain flour
½ cup brown sugar
½ cup desiccated coconut
125 g butter, melted

Chocolate Topping
200 g dark cooking chocolate
2 tbsp oil (e.g. rice bran or canola)
½–¾ tsp rock or flaky salt, to taste

Caramel Filling
⅔ cup golden syrup
125 g butter
2 x 395 g tins sweetened condensed milk
½–¾ cup crunchy peanut butter (make sure it's the kind with salt)

1 Preheat oven to 180°C. Grease and line a tin with baking paper.

2 Place flour, sugar, coconut and melted butter in a bowl and mix well.

3 Press mix into lined tin. Bake for 12–16 minutes or until light golden brown.

4 To make the caramel filling, place golden syrup, butter and condensed milk in a medium pot and stir over a low heat until butter is melted — I find a silicone spatula to be the best thing for this as it stops the caramel sticking and burning.

5 Continue to stir for 7–10 minutes until caramel has thickened slightly and comes away from the side of the pot.

6 Stir in ½ cup peanut butter until smooth. Taste caramel and add more peanut butter, if desired. Pour hot caramel over base.

7 Bake for 8–12 minutes until caramel starts to brown on top (watch carefully during the last few minutes of cooking!).

8 Cool on bench, then refrigerate until cold.

9 Melt together chocolate and oil until smooth and pour over cold slice. Leave to set for a few minutes (no more than 5 minutes), then sprinkle over rock or flaky salt to taste.

10 Put slice back in fridge until chocolate is set, then remove from tin and cut into small squares with a large sharp knife. To get a clean, sharp cut, run your knife under hot water and wipe dry every two to three slices.

Baker's Note — Measuring Golden Syrup Accurately

Measuring golden syrup accurately can be a messy business so heat a metal spoon in hot water when measuring in spoonfuls. When the recipe calls for cup measures, spray your measuring cup with non-stick baking spray and pour syrup into cup up to required amount. Both methods allow the golden syrup to slide right into your bowl, which means you get a perfect measure.

Peppermint Fudge
Brownie

Rich and chocolatey with a big hit of peppermint, this is dessert brownie at its best. Serve after dinner with a cup of coffee or a wee tipple of liqueur.

Makes 16 pieces

250 g butter
½ cup cocoa
1½ cups sugar
4 eggs
1 tsp vanilla extract
1 cup plain flour

1 tsp baking powder
¼ tsp salt
100 g dark chocolate, chopped
400 g (2 packets) Cadbury's After Dinner Mints

1   Preheat oven to 170°C. Grease and line a 23 cm square cake tin.

2   Melt butter over a low heat, then whisk in cocoa.

3   Remove from heat, stir in sugar then whisk in eggs, one at a time. Add vanilla and stir well.

4   Fold in flour, baking powder and salt until just combined, then fold in chopped chocolate.

5   Pour half the batter into the prepared tin and spread out evenly.

6   Top batter with after dinner mints, placing them as close together as possible. Pour over remaining batter.

7   Bake for 30–35 minutes or until brownie starts to look cooked around the edges but is still a bit wobbly in the middle. Cool in tin on a wire rack.

Baker's Note — After Dinner Mints
You could replace the after dinner mints with 1 tsp peppermint essence, if you wish, but the inclusion of the mints adds a lovely chewy layer to the bottom of the brownie as they cook and melt into the brownie mix, so it's well worth the expense for a special occasion.

Almond
Croissants

Almond croissants were invented as a way of using up croissants that didn't sell and, sacrilege though it may be, I think they're even better this way. So next time you have overnight guests, plan ahead and buy croissants a day or two early so you can whip up these hedonistic treats for an incredibly easy but very impressive breakfast.

Makes 4

¼ cup boiling water
1 tbsp caster sugar
4 stale croissants (1–3 days old is best)

Filling
100 g caster sugar
100 g blanched almonds

¼ tsp salt
100 g butter
2 eggs
70 g sliced almonds

icing sugar, to serve

1   Preheat oven to 180°C. Line a baking tray with baking paper.

2   Make a syrup by combining boiling water and sugar and stir until sugar has dissolved. Split croissants through the middle and set aside.

3   To make the filling, place sugar, blanched almonds and salt in a food processor and pulse until finely ground. Add butter and mix well. Add eggs and mix to a creamy paste.

4   Brush syrup over tops, bottoms and sides of croissants.

5   Put a generous couple of tablespoons of the almond paste on the bottom half of each croissant and place the top half back on. Press down lightly and spread more almond paste on the top. Press sliced almonds all over the top.

6   Bake for 15 minutes or until almonds are golden brown and croissants are crispy. Dust with icing sugar and serve immediately.

Baker's Note — Butter or Margarine
Try to source good-quality croissants from a French bakery rather than using croissants from the supermarket. Often supermarket croissants are made with margarine, not butter, and the taste and texture are vastly inferior to proper buttery, flaky croissants.

Variations
Pain au chocolat can be made into a great almond croissant and adds an extra dimension of naughtiness.

Chocolate
Brioches

Brioche is heavenly fresh out of the oven for morning tea. To save having to get up at the crack of dawn to make it, make the dough up to the end of Step 6 and leave overnight in the fridge. Even though these brioches look like pastries, they owe more to bread-making than pastry-making (see page 76 before you start this recipe).

Makes 12

4 cups high grade flour
2 tsp salt
6 eggs
70 ml milk, at room temperature
4 tsp bread maker yeast
350 g butter, cubed, at room temperature
2 tbsp caster sugar

Ganache
200 g dark chocolate
150 ml cream

Egg Wash
1 egg yolk
1 tbsp milk

1   Place the flour, salt and eggs in the bowl of a stand mixer fitted with the dough hook. Add the milk and yeast and mix on low speed until well combined (about 5 minutes).

2   Scrape down the sides of the bowl with a rubber spatula, then knead on medium for 10 minutes. Dough should be smooth, elastic and well combined.

3   Combine the butter and sugar in another bowl and, with the mixer on a low speed, add a few chunks to the dough. Keep adding butter, a piece at a time, until it is all incorporated.

4   Increase the mixer speed to medium and mix for 6–10 minutes until dough is very smooth and shiny and comes away from the sides of the bowl.

5   Tip dough into a lightly oiled bowl and leave in a warm spot to double in size (about 2 hours).

6   Knock back the dough, cover again and refrigerate until required (at least 6 or up to 24 hours).

7   Make the ganache by heating the chocolate and cream in a microwave in short bursts on high or in a bowl over a pot of simmering water. Stir until combined, cover and cool to room temperature.

8   Remove dough from fridge and roll out to a 25 cm x 45 cm rectangle (long side towards you) and spread with ganache. Roll up dough to form a long log and cut into 12 even-sized pieces.

9   Lightly grease two 6-hole large muffin tins (or line with baking paper or muffin cases, if you wish) and place a piece of dough in each. Shape the dough slightly to remove any corners or edges before you put them in.

10   Cover and place in a warm spot to rise for 1½ hours or until doubled in size.

11   Make egg wash by lightly whisking together egg yolk and milk.

12 Preheat oven to 200°C. Once the brioches have risen, carefully brush the tops with egg wash.

13 Bake for 15–20 minutes until golden brown and well risen. Leave in the tin for a few minutes before inverting onto a wire rack to cool. If there's any chocolate left in the bottom, spoon it back onto the brioches. Try not to eat them all at once!

Variations

Try white chocolate chunks and raspberries or dark chocolate and blueberries. A savoury brioche can be made by filling the dough with spinach, sundried tomato, feta and prosciutto — or any combination of 'bits' you can think of. Try a good-quality Cheddar with relish for a lunchtime combination.

Cinnamon Pull-apart
Bread

This loaf is great to share and the very form of it, with 'leaves' of lovely soft cinnamon sugar-smeared dough, encourages you to dive right in and tear off a piece. So that you can enjoy it mid-morning (without having to get up before the birds), make the dough up to the end of Step 4, knock it back, then cover with plastic wrap and store in the fridge overnight. Bring it back to room temperature (see Baker's Note on page 143) before carrying on with the next step.

Serves 4–6

Dough
60 g butter
⅓ cup milk
¼ cup water
2 tsp vanilla extract
2½ cups high grade flour
3 tsp bread maker yeast
¼ cup sugar
½ tsp salt
2 large eggs, at room temperature
¼ cup flour extra, plus flour for dusting

Filling
½ cup brown sugar
2 tsp ground cinnamon
1 tsp ground mixed spice
60 g butter, melted

Caramel Glaze
½ cup icing sugar, sifted
2 tbsp caramel sauce or 1 tsp caramel essence
water

1   To make the dough, warm butter and milk together until butter melts. Stir in the water and vanilla extract and set aside.

2   In the bowl of a stand mixer (or a just a large bowl, if you're making by hand), put the first measure of flour, yeast, sugar and salt. Add milk mixture and stir until just combined. With mixer on low, add eggs, one at a time, mixing well after each addition.

3   Touch the dough and if it really sticks to your fingers, add flour, two tablespoons at a time, mixing well after each addition, until it is only a little sticky.

4   Knead dough for 7 minutes, if using a mixer, or 12 minutes if making by hand — it will still be very soft and sticky but should also be smooth and satiny. Place the dough in a large, clean, lightly oiled bowl, cover with plastic wrap and leave to rise in a warm spot until doubled in size (1–2 hours).

5   Preheat oven to 170°C. Grease a 10 cm x 22 cm loaf tin.

6   Once bread has risen, tip out onto a lightly floured bench and roll out to a 50 cm x 30 cm rectangle. Use a ruler to make sure you have the right size.

7   To make the filling, mix together the sugar and spices. Brush the melted butter over the dough, making sure it is completely covered, then sprinkle the sugar mix evenly over the butter.

8   Using a sharp knife, cut the dough into five 10 cm x 30 cm strips. Carefully stack the strips on top of each other (don't worry if the dough stretches a little as you pick it up; just kind of shimmy it back together), then cut the stack into six 10 cm x 5 cm rectangles.

9   Carefully transfer the dough pieces to your loaf tin, cut-sides up, and side by side. There may still be a little room in the tin, but this will disappear as the dough expands during rising and baking.

10 Loosely cover the pan with plastic wrap and leave to rise in a warm spot until almost doubled in size (30–50 minutes).

11 Bake for 30–40 minutes, checking after 15 minutes to make sure the top isn't browning too quickly. If it is, cover it loosely with tin foil. When the loaf is brown on top and cooked, transfer to a wire rack for 10 minutes before turning out.

12 While the loaf is baking, make the glaze by mixing together the icing sugar and caramel sauce or essence with just enough water to make it fall off the spoon in a thin ribbon. Drizzle the still warm loaf with the glaze and dig in!

Baker's Note — Bringing Dough Back to Room Temperature

Use your oven to bring dough back to room temperature after it has been in the fridge. Turn the oven to its lowest setting and cover your dough with a damp tea towel. Check the dough every 20 minutes until it is back to room temperature.

Variation — Lemon Citrus Pull-apart Bread

Try mixing the zest of 4 lemons with the zest of 1 orange and ½ cup sugar and use in place of the brown sugar and cinnamon mix. Make a simple lemon icing by mixing ½ cup icing sugar, 1 tbsp lemon juice and water, then drizzle over the bread in place of the caramel glaze.

Daring

Bacon with chocolate, apple with cheese, pinot noir with blackberries, and quinoa with orange blossom water are just some of the more exotic combinations of ingredients included in this chapter. Some recipes have ingredients that are not usually included in baking; others have more difficult techniques or require some specialised equipment, but each one is carefully chosen to both challenge your skills and creativity, and delight your palate.

Make Swiss Meringue Buttercream

If you've never tried Swiss meringue buttercream before, you'll be blown away by this not-too-sweet, dreamy, creamy, amazingly light and tasty frosting. It's nothing like traditional buttercream in taste, texture or sweetness and is much more grown-up for it. One thing to note: always serve it at room temperature or all you will taste is the butter.

Makes about 5 cups (enough to generously ice 12 cupcakes or a single-layer cake)

450 g butter, cold
5 egg whites
1½ cups caster sugar

½ tsp salt
1 tbsp vanilla extract

1   Remove butter from the fridge and cut into chunks about the size of a tablespoon. Leave on the bench to soften while you prepare the meringue.

2   Place egg whites and sugar in a bowl over a pot of simmering water and whisk continuously until sugar is dissolved (about 5 minutes). To check, you can use a thermometer (it should read 70°C) or rub a bit of egg white between your thumb and finger. It should be hot and you shouldn't be able to feel any grains of sugar.

3   Pour egg whites into the bowl of a stand mixer and, with whisk attached, beat on high until cool (about 10 minutes). It's important that the outside of the bowl feels neutral to the touch (not warm), otherwise the butter will melt when you beat it in.

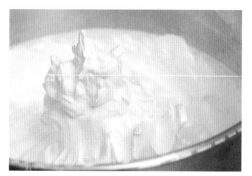

4 Swap the whisk attachment for the paddle attachment and add butter, one chunk at a time, beating very well on low after each addition.

5 Once all the butter is incorporated, beat until it reaches a silky smooth texture. If the mixture curdles, keep on beating and it will come back. If the mixture is too runny, place in the fridge for 15 minutes, then continue beating with the paddle attachment. It may help to add a couple more chunks of cold butter, too.

6 Beat in salt and vanilla, then add any other flavours or colours as per your recipe and beat well.

Baker's Note — Storing Swiss Meringue Buttercream

Keep in airtight container in the fridge for up to one week. Let it reach room temperature again when you need it and rewhip with the paddle attachment in an electric mixer to get it back to the right consistency. It will freeze for up to 6–8 weeks. To thaw, leave out overnight and rewhip for 5 minutes as above.

If buttercream still doesn't have its lovely satiny finish after rewhipping, microwave about one-third of it on high for about 10 seconds, then add back into remaining buttercream in mixer bowl, beating for a few moments to incorporate.

Variations

Chocolate — Beat in 250 g melted dark chocolate.
Berry or fruit — Beat in ½ cup berry or fruit pureé.
Vanilla — Beat in an extra tablespoon of vanilla extract.

Pinot Noir

Cupcakes

For these deliciously grown-up cupcakes I use a local wine, Te Tera Pinot Noir, from the award-winning winemakers at Martinborough Vineyard. If you're unable to get hold of this fine drop, then substitute another good (Martinborough!) Pinot Noir.

Makes 24 cupcakes

Berry Mixture
1½ cups cherries, tinned or fresh, pitted and
    drained
1½ cups blackberries, fresh or frozen
1 cup Te Tera Pinot Noir
1 tbsp sugar

Cupcakes
1⅔ cups plain flour
1½ cups sugar
¾ cup cocoa
¾ tsp baking soda
¼ tsp salt

185 g butter, melted
3 eggs
1½ tsp vanilla extract
1½ cups berry mixture

Swiss Meringue Buttercream
650 g butter, cold
7 eggs whites
2 cups caster sugar
¼ tsp salt
¾ cup berry mixture

24 blackberries, to decorate

1   To make the berry mixture, stir together in a medium glass or ceramic bowl (not plastic or metal) the cherries, blackberries, wine and sugar and leave to soak in the fridge for at least 2 hours (or overnight). Process in a blender in short bursts until well combined and liquefied.

2   Preheat oven to 170°C. Line two 12-hole muffin tins with cupcake cases.

3   To make the cupcakes, stir together flour, sugar, cocoa, baking soda and salt in the bowl of a stand mixer on its lowest setting.

4   Add melted butter, eggs and vanilla and beat on a medium speed for 1 minute. Add 1½ cups berry mixture and beat for 20 seconds.

5   Two-thirds fill cupcake cases with batter. Bake for 16–20 minutes or until cupcakes spring back when lightly touched. Cool on a wire rack.

6   To make frosting, add ¾ cup berry mixture in at the final step (see page 147) and mix well to combine.

7   Pipe generous swirls of frosting on top of cooled cupcakes and finish with a blackberry.

Baker's Note — Berry Mixture

You will have about a cup of the berry mixture left over after making your frosting. Put it to good use on ice cream, pancakes or as extra sauce on your cupcakes — it will keep in a sealed container in the fridge for a few weeks. If you'd prefer not to taste the alcohol, simmer the berry mixture over a medium heat for 5 minutes to cook off the alcohol.

Triple Chocolate Cupcakes
with Beer

The addition of beer to these rich, chocolatey cupcakes adds a new dimension of flavour. Craftsman Chocolate Oatmeal Stout (see Baker's Note on page 151) is the perfect brew to use, but you could also try Guinness or another very rich stout.

Makes 18 cupcakes

250 ml Craftsman Chocolate Oatmeal Stout
250 g butter, cubed
¾ cup cocoa
1¾ cups caster sugar
½ cup sour cream
2 eggs
1 tbsp vanilla extract
2¼ cups plain flour
2¼ tsp baking soda

Frosting
250 ml Craftsman Chocolate Oatmeal Stout
1 tbsp sugar
500 g cream cheese, at room temperature
125 g butter, softened
1 tsp vanilla extract
4 cups icing sugar

Ganache
250 g dark chocolate
½ cup cream

1   Preheat oven to 180°C. Line two 12-hole muffin tins with 18 cupcake cases.

2   Place beer in a large saucepan and add butter. Heat over a medium heat until butter is melted, stirring occasionally. Whisk in cocoa and sugar.

3   In a small bowl, beat together sour cream, eggs and vanilla extract, then pour into the beer mixture. Whisk in flour and baking soda.

4   Two-thirds fill cupcake cases with the batter. Bake for 15–20 minutes or until cupcakes spring back when lightly touched. Cool in tins for 3 minutes before turning out onto a wire rack to cool completely.

5   To make the frosting, place beer and sugar in a small saucepan and simmer gently until beer is reduced to about 3 tablespoons. It may seem to take ages to start reducing, but once it does it'll happen in a hurry so watch it carefully.

6   Beat cream cheese and butter until light and fluffy. Add beer reduction and vanilla extract and beat until smooth. Add icing sugar and beat again until light and fluffy. Chill for 1–2 hours before icing cupcakes.

7   Make the ganache by heating the chocolate and cream in a microwave in short bursts on high, or in a bowl over a pot of simmering water. Stir until combined and set aside to cool to room temperature.

8   To assemble, pipe or slather a generous amount of frosting on top of cooled cupcakes and top with a spoonful of ganache.

Baker's Note — Craftsman Chocolate Oatmeal Stout

I stumbled across Renaissance Brewing Company's Craftsman Chocolate Oatmeal Stout at the New Zealand Chocolate Festival and it turns out that beer and chocolate are a great pairing. This beer works particularly well because it is brewed using cocoa nibs, which add wonderful chocolatey notes to it. Find it online or at your local supermarket.

Variation

You can make this as one 20 cm ring cake as well. Make as directed, baking for 25–30 minutes during the first bake and another 10–15 minutes once the syrup and almonds have been added.

Moroccan Mint and Honey *Cakes*

These lovely moist little cakes are lush with the smell and taste of fresh mint and honey. Serve with honey-sweetened yoghurt and mint tea, and relax on a pile of cushions for an indulgent Moroccan-style treat.

Makes 6 cakes

Mint Syrup
130 ml water
½ cup sugar
1 cup roughly chopped fresh mint

Honeyed Almonds
50 g butter
½ cup honey
120 g sliced almonds

Cakes
1 cup plain flour
1 tsp baking powder
¼ tsp salt
150 g desiccated coconut
100 g butter, softened
200 g sugar
1 tbsp chopped fresh mint
4 eggs

1   Preheat oven to 150°C. Line a 6-hole large muffin tin with baking paper or pre-folded muffin papers.

2   To make the mint syrup, place the water, sugar and mint in small pot and bring to the boil, stirring occasionally to dissolve the sugar. Remove from heat and cool to room temperature. Strain through a sieve and discard mint leaves.

3   To make the cakes, whisk together flour, baking powder, salt and coconut in a small bowl.

4   Beat the butter, sugar and mint until it just starts to pale. Add 1 egg and a quarter of the flour mixture and beat well. Repeat with remaining eggs and flour.

5   Divide batter evenly between muffin tins. Bake for 20 minutes.

6   While the cakes are baking, make the honeyed almonds by heating all ingredients in a small pot over a low heat, stirring constantly. Do not allow to boil.

7   When cakes have been in oven 20 minutes, remove and prick the tops all over with a long wooden skewer. Pour over mint syrup, allowing it to soak in well.

8   Top with hot honeyed almonds and return to the oven for another 10–12 minutes or until almonds are a light brown colour.

9   Cool in tins for 15 minutes before removing and serving immediately.

Angel Food Cake with
Rosewater and Strawberries

Angel food cake is so called because it's so light it might float away and because it's very low in fat. It's very popular in America and can be used as a base for a number of different flavours (see Variations on page 155). Here I've used strawberries, white chocolate and a touch of rosewater for an exotic twist on a familiar flavour combination.

Serves 10–12

1 cup plain flour	**Rosewater Syrup**	**To Finish**
¾ cup caster sugar,	1 cup water	300 ml cream
plus ½ cup extra	½ cup sugar	1 tsp rosewater
12 egg whites	4 tsp lemon juice	2 punnets strawberries
1 tsp cream of tartar	1 tsp rosewater	75–100 g white chocolate,
¼ tsp salt		grated
2 tsp vanilla extract		

1 Preheat oven to 160°C. Have ready a clean, dry angel food cake tin. *Do not* grease, flour or line in any way (see Baker's Note on page 155).

2 Sift together flour and ¾ cup caster sugar and set aside.

3 Beat egg whites, cream of tartar and salt until soft peaks form. Slowly add ½ cup caster sugar, beating all the while. Beat until thick and glossy.

4 Turn the mixer to low and add vanilla, then carefully fold in sifted flour and sugar.

5 Spoon batter into the tin and bang it down on the bench a couple of times to remove any air pockets.

6 Bake for 35–40 minutes until dry-textured and golden brown. When you remove it from the oven, immediately turn it upside down, leaving it in the tin to cool. Leave like this until cold.

7 While the cake is cooling, make the rosewater syrup by bringing the water and sugar to the boil, stirring until sugar has dissolved. Boil for 5 minutes, remove from heat and stir in lemon juice and rosewater. Set aside to cool.

8 When cake is completely cold, unmould it by running a knife around the edge of the cake and carefully lifting it off the base. Use a serrated knife to slice it horizontally into three equal layers.

9 Whip cream with rosewater to medium peaks and slice hulled strawberries.

10 To assemble, place the bottom layer of the cake on a serving plate and brush with a generous portion of the rosewater syrup. Top with whipped cream and sliced strawberries. Repeat with other layers, adding grated chocolate on top of the last layer. Serve immediately.

Baker's Note — Angel Food Cake Tins

Angel food cake tins are special non-stick tins that have a raised hole in the middle or little 'legs' on the side to hold the cake up above the bench when it is turned upside-down after baking (this stops the cake from deflating). Never grease, spray or line an angel food cake tin as the batter needs to be able to 'climb' the sides to get a good rise. Tins can be found at any good kitchen store or online at Jessica Design Store.

Variations

Make a chocolate angel food cake by adding ¼ cup cocoa to the flour and reducing the flour to ¾ cup. You can also make it gluten-free by using gluten-free flour. It's great served plain with fresh berries and ice cream, or lemon curd and sorbet.

Chocolate and Bacon *Cupcakes*

This may seem like an odd combination but if you're a fan of sweet and salty, these will really hit the spot. The cupcakes are light and fluffy with a hint of salt from the bacon and the frosting creamy and sweet. Don't tell people what they're eating until after the first bite and they'll be stunned by the deliciousness of the combination.

Makes 24 cupcakes

⅔ cup cocoa
⅔ cup boiling water
2¼ cups plain flour
¾ tsp baking soda
¾ tsp baking powder
1 tsp salt
225 g butter
1½ cups brown sugar
3 eggs
1 tbsp vanilla extract

¾ cup buttermilk
¾ cup finely chopped cooked bacon

Maple Frosting
250 g butter
2 tsp vanilla extract
⅓ cup maple syrup, plus extra for drizzling
1 tsp salt
3⅓ cups icing sugar, sifted

1   Preheat oven to 170°C and line two 12-hole muffin tins with cupcake cases.

2   In a small bowl, whisk together the cocoa and boiling water until smooth. Set aside.

3   In another bowl, whisk together the flour, baking soda, baking powder and salt. Set aside.

4   In a small pot over a medium heat, melt together the butter and sugar until combined. Pour into the bowl of a stand mixer and beat on medium speed until cool (4–5 minutes).

5   Add eggs to the butter and sugar, one at a time, beating well after each addition. Beat in vanilla extract, then the dissolved cocoa.

6   Fold in half of the flour, then half the buttermilk. Repeat with remaining flour and buttermilk, then fold in cooked, chopped bacon.

7   Three-quarters fill cupcake cases with the batter.

8   Bake for 20 minutes or until cupcakes spring back when lightly touched. When cooked, leave cupcakes in tins for 3 minutes before removing to wire racks to cool completely.

9   While the cupcakes cool, make the frosting. Beat the butter until light and fluffy, then beat in the vanilla extract, maple syrup and salt. Beat in the icing sugar, one cup at a time. Taste and add more maple syrup, if desired.

10   To serve, pipe or spoon a generous dollop of frosting on top of cooled cupcakes and drizzle with extra maple syrup.

Baker's Note — Quality Bacon and Maple Syrup

As usual, the quality of your ingredients really makes a difference in this recipe. Don't skimp on the quality of either the bacon or the maple syrup. Choose high-quality, free-range (if you can), flavoursome bacon. I like to use streaky bacon as you may as well go, well, er … the whole hog. And it goes without saying that you should use pure real maple syrup — maple 'flavoured' syrup just won't cut the mustard.

Variation

These cupcakes are still delicious in their 'naked' form. In fact, I have been known to skip the frosting altogether and just eat them straight from the oven. So if the thought of adding more sugar, butter and other assorted 'bad things' makes your arteries shrivel in horror, try the 'low calorie version' (cough, cough) and hold the frosting.

Assemble Layer Cakes

There are few things more impressive than cutting into a cake to find it made up of many different layers.

2 or more cake layers
icing and fillings

Tools
board or plate, to put cake on
long serrated knife (or cake leveller)

large straight-edged metal spatula or knife
small straight-edged metal spatula or knife (or
   offset spatula)
small bowl, for raising cake board off the bench
   (or a cake turntable)

1   Firstly, you need to trim any domes off the cakes. You can buy cake levellers, but the easiest way to do this is to use a large serrated knife and a small object (the same height as you want the cake to be) as a knife rest. I use a tiny upturned glass bowl.

2   Place your cake on the bench (or a cake turntable) and place the object beside it. Rest the knife flat on the object and slice into the cake — only go the depth of the knife, not all the way in. Rotate the cake and continue slicing inwards to the depth of the knife until you've gone all the way around the cake. Go back around the cake slicing a bit deeper (but not all the way through).

3   Cut an X across the middle of the cake, down to the depth of your horizontal cut, then cut off each quarter. You may need to do a little more levelling to get a flat surface.

4   Repeat with other layers.

5   Place the bottom layer of your cake bottom side-down on board (or directly onto your plate) and place on a cake turntable or on an upside-down bowl. Use a small blob of icing to 'glue' the bottom layer to the board if you're worried about it shifting.

6   Spread over any filling (jam, curd, etc.) that you're using, then plonk on ½–1 cup icing. Use a small spatula (offset, if you have it) to evenly spread the icing over the surface of the cake. Push the icing slightly over the edges as you go.

7   Repeat with the middle layer(s) of cake, pressing down lightly to even it out before you apply the icing.

8   When you get to the top layer, place it cut side-down so you have a smooth surface to work with.

9   Place about 1½ cups icing on top of the cake and, using a spatula, spread the icing, plus any oozing out from between the layers, to create a 'crumb coat'. Don't spend too much time trying to make it look good — the crumb coat is just to seal in the crumbs so they don't mar the outside of the cake.

10   Refrigerate the cake for 15 minutes (or longer) to set the crumb coat.

11 Using a large spatula, generously coat the
chilled cake with icing. Smooth the top of
the cake first. Hold the long edge of the
spatula to the top of the cake at a 45-degree
angle and slowly rotate the turntable. If the
icing appears to be streaky or is difficult to
smooth, dip the spatula into hot water, wipe
it dry, then continue spreading.

12 Smooth out the sides using the large knife or
offset spatula, and holding the knife vertically
at a 45-degree angle to the side of the cake.

13 Smooth the edge where the sides meet the top by running the flat edge of your small spatula or
knife around the cake.

14 Finish decorating as desired.

Baker's Note — Sourcing Equipment

Cake turntables, spatulas, cake levellers, gel food colouring and decorations can be found at
any good kitchenware or cake decorating store. There are a number of online stores here in
New Zealand that specialise in cake decorating. They have a wide variety of specialist tools, are
incredibly knowledgeable and are very helpful, to boot.

See page 192 for Celebration Cake recipe (opposite)

Red Velvet
Cheesecake

When I asked my friend Hayley what she wanted for a birthday cake, she had trouble deciding between a red velvet cake and a baked cheesecake. She eventually decided on the cake but, figuring both couldn't be a bad thing, I came up with a combination which is absolutely amazing and completely worth the effort.

Serves 12–14

Cheesecake
500 g cream cheese, at room temperature
⅔ cup caster sugar
2 tbsp plain flour
3 eggs
½ cup cream
1 tsp vanilla extract

½ tsp salt
2 eggs
1½ cups vegetable oil
1 cup buttermilk
50 ml red food colouring
3 tsp vanilla extract
2 tsp white vinegar

Red Velvet Cake
2½ cups plain flour
1½ cups sugar
4 tbsp cocoa
1½ tsp baking soda

Cream Cheese Frosting
500 g cream cheese, at room temperature
125 g butter, softened
1 tbsp lemon juice
2½–3 cups icing sugar

1 Preheat oven to 160°C. Line the base of a 23 cm round spring-form cake tin with baking paper and grease the sides really well.

2 To make the cheesecake, beat the cream cheese in the bowl of a stand mixer until light and fluffy. Beat in the sugar and flour, then add the eggs, one at a time, beating well after each addition. Stir in cream and vanilla extract.

3 Pour into prepared tin and place in the oven with a large dish of hot water on the rack below the cheesecake.

4 Bake for 30–35 minutes or until cheesecake only has a small wobble in the middle. Cool in tin, then freeze completely (at least 6 hours, but preferably overnight) until required.

5 To make the cakes, increase oven to 175°C and grease and line two 23 cm round cake tins.

6 In the bowl of a stand mixer, stir together flour, sugar, cocoa, baking soda and salt.

7 Add eggs, oil, buttermilk, food colouring, vanilla and vinegar and use a spoon to stir together until combined (this saves you having to clean red food colouring off your ceiling). Once combined, turn on the mixer and beat on medium-low for 1 minute until smooth.

8 Divide batter evenly between prepared tins (weigh them if you can).

9   Bake for 30–35 minutes or until a skewer inserted in the middle comes out clean. Cool in tins for 10 minutes before turning out onto wire racks to cool completely.

10 To make the frosting, beat the cream cheese and butter in a stand mixer until light and fluffy. Beat in lemon juice, then add 2½ cups icing sugar. Beat until fluffy, then add more icing sugar if it seems too soft.

11 To assemble cake (see page 158 for detailed instructions), level the cooled cakes and place one cake on your serving plate or cake stand.

12 Place the frozen cheesecake layer on top, then top with the other levelled cake.

13 Use about 1 cup of the frosting to make a crumb coating on the outside of the cake. Chill for 15 minutes, then smooth over the remaining frosting.

14 Leave to stand for 20–30 minutes (so that the cheesecake centre has time to soften) before serving.

Baker's Note — Red Velvet Cake

If you've never made red velvet cake before, then the quantity of food colouring is likely to give you a mild heart attack. All I can say is that it's just not the same if the colour isn't a deep, dark red so just go with it — it's not like you eat it every day. Also, with this cake it's really important that you use buttermilk, not a buttermilk substitute, as it's this which gives the cake its lovely velvety crumb.

Coconut Cloud Cake with Passion Fruit Curd

This is a special occasion cake for coconut-lovers. The sweet, cloud-like frosting hides a cake full of coconut flavour with a wonderful texture and the passion fruit curd hidden inside gives it a wonderful tropical tartness.

Serves 10–12

6 egg whites (reserve yolks for curd)
1½ cups coconut milk
1½ tsp vanilla extract
1 tsp coconut essence
3½ cups plain flour
2 cups caster sugar
5 tsp baking powder
1 tsp salt
225 g coconut oil (see Baker's Note on page 165)

Passion Fruit Curd
150 g butter
¾ cup caster sugar
zest and juice of 3 lemons
6 egg yolks
½ cup passion fruit pulp (4–5 passion fruit)

Cloud Frosting
2 egg whites
1 cup caster sugar
¼ cup cold water
¼ tsp cream of tartar
2 tbsp flaked or shredded coconut

1   Preheat oven to 170°C and put one rack in the lower third of the oven and another in the upper third. Grease the sides and line the bases of two 23 cm round cake tins.

2   In a medium bowl, whisk together egg whites, ⅓ cup coconut milk, vanilla extract and coconut essence and set aside.

3   In the bowl of a stand electric mixer, place flour, sugar, baking powder and salt and mix on low for 30 seconds to combine.

4   Add coconut oil and remaining coconut milk and mix on low until combined. Increase speed to medium and mix for another 1½ minutes.

5   Scrape down the sides of the bowl and add one-third of the egg white mixture. Beat on medium-low for 20 seconds, scrape down sides and repeat with another third of the egg whites. Repeat again with remaining third.

6   Divide batter evenly between prepared cake tins.

7   Bake for 30–40 minutes, swapping tins around at the 25-minute mark. Cool in tins for 10 minutes before turning out onto a wire rack to cool completely.

8   To make the curd, melt the butter in a heavy-based saucepan over a medium heat. Remove from heat and whisk in sugar, lemon zest and juice and egg yolks. Return to heat, whisking continuously until curd thickens. Cool to room temperature, then stir in passion fruit and refrigerate. Curd will thicken considerably in the fridge.

9   To make the cloud frosting, place the egg whites, sugar, water and cream of tartar in a bowl over a saucepan of simmering water. Whisk continually until sugar has dissolved (about 5 minutes), then pour into the bowl of a stand mixer. Beat with whisk attachment on medium for 7 minutes.

10 To assemble, place one cake on a large serving plate, top with a good quantity of curd (you won't need all of it so pop the rest back in the fridge). Top with the other cake, then spread frosting generously all over sides and top. Use a spatula to make upward stripes that finish in peaks and top with coconut. Serve immediately.

Baker's Note — Coconut Oil

Coconut oil is a great alternative to butter and can be used in any recipe in pretty much the same way. It can be found shelved with the other oils in your local supermarket; however, as it's a solid, look for a small tub or jar rather than a bottle.

To measure, use a spoon or knife to scrape thin layers off the top of the coconut oil and place in a bowl to weigh. Thin layers are best because they immediately soften to the perfect consistency for baking.

Pear Cake with Quince and Pinot Gris *Jelly*

There's something about this cake, topped with glistening chunks of boozy jelly, that makes it irresistible. The cake itself is soft and spicy, the frosting creamy and smooth and the jelly gives it a very adult kick. I've used the 2010 Burnt Spur Pinot Gris from Martinborough for this cake (see Baker's Note on page 167).

Serves 8–10

4 pears, peeled, cored and diced
1 cup Pinot Gris
125 g butter
1 cup sugar
½ cup honey
2 eggs
1 tsp vanilla extract
2 cups plain flour
1½ tsp baking soda
½ tsp salt
½ tsp ground cardamom
1 tsp ground cinnamon

Jelly
4½ tsp gelatine
¼ cup water
1 cup pinot gris
½ cup reserved pear liquid (from cake)
sugar, to taste
120 g quince paste

1 recipe Swiss meringue buttercream (see page 146)

1 Simmer pears and wine over a medium heat until pears are very soft. Strain through a sieve, reserving liquid, and then mash pears. Set aside to cool.

2 Preheat oven to 180°C. Grease and line a 20 cm round cake tin.

3 Cream butter and sugar until light and fluffy. Beat in honey. Add eggs and vanilla and beat well. Mix in flour, baking soda, salt, cardamom and cinnamon. Fold in mashed pears.

4 Spoon into prepared tin. Bake for 40–50 minutes or until a skewer inserted in the middle comes out with just a few crumbs attached. Cool in the tin for 10 minutes before turning out onto a wire rack to cool completely.

5 To make the jelly, sprinkle the gelatine over the water, stir well with a fork and set aside. In a saucepan, heat the wine and reserved pear liquid to a simmer, then whisk in sugar (if needed), quince paste and gelatine until smooth. Pour into a very clean 20 cm x 30 cm sponge roll tin and place in the fridge until firm.

6 Make the Swiss meringue buttercream (see page 146).

7   To assemble the cake, cover the outside in a good thick layer of buttercream. Soak a tea towel in hot water and wring out. Spread over the bench and place jelly tray on top (this will help loosen the jelly). Tip the jelly upside-down onto a large piece of baking paper (don't worry if it breaks) and slice into squares about 5 mm x 5 mm.

8   Sprinkle the jelly over the top of the iced cake and press a few pieces into the sides. Serve immediately.

Baker's Note — Wine and Flavour Matching

The flavours for this cake (pear and quince) were drawn from the amazing 2010 Burnt Spur Pinot Gris and marry perfectly with each other. When you're choosing a wine for this cake, read the label to see what flavours it has and try matching them with the fruit and fruit paste you use.

Make Sweet Pastry

I'm the first person to reach for the bought pastry when it comes to making tarts and pies, but every now and then I feel virtuous and make it from scratch. This is a great, simple recipe that keeps well wrapped in the fridge for up to five days and in the freezer for up to a month. The variations (see page 171) are a great way to tailor the pastry to the filling.

Makes about 500 g

2 cups high grade flour
⅔ cup icing sugar
¼ tsp salt

100 g butter, cubed and slightly softened
2 eggs

1   In a large bowl, combine flour, sugar and salt and, using only your fingertips, rub in the butter until it resembles very coarse breadcrumbs — you want different-sized lumps of butter in the mix as it's the lumps of butter that create the flakiness. If you want to do this part in a food processor you can, but use the pulse function for only a few seconds at a time, checking between pulses.

2   Add eggs and, again using only your fingertips, work them in until the dough begins to hold together.

3   Tip the dough out onto the bench and knead lightly, using the palm of your hands. Push the dough across the bench with the palm of your hand, then use a bench scraper or a knife to gather it back up into a ball. Rotate 180 degrees and repeat. The dough should be smooth, but with a few small pieces of butter showing through.

4   Form pastry into a ball, flatten into a circle about 1.5 cm high and wrap in plastic wrap. Chill for at least 1 hour (preferably 2 hours) before using as per your recipe's instructions.

Baker's Note — Using Only Egg Yolks

If you're topping your pie with meringue, substitute the 2 whole eggs in the pastry recipe for 4 egg yolks. You may need to add a tablespoon or so of iced water to bring the pastry together.

Variations

For almond pastry — Reduce flour to 1½ cups and add ½ cup ground almonds. Great with tarts filed with pastry cream and topped with fruit.

For lemon-scented pastry — Add the finely grated zest of 1 lemon with the eggs. Great with apple and other fruit pies.

For vanilla pastry — Add 1 tsp vanilla extract with the eggs. Perfect with chocolate or caramel meringue pies.

Gin and Tonic Tart

This is a great grown-up twist on a lemon tart as it brings together the best of both a cocktail and a dessert. Perfect served courtside after a rousing game of tennis, with lashings of whipped cream and a long cool drink!

Serves 8–10

Pastry
200 g high grade flour
¼ cup icing sugar
zest of 1 lemon, finely grated
75 g cold butter, cut into cubes
1 egg yolk
¼ cup cold tonic water

Syrup
⅓ cup caster sugar
½ cup tonic water
juice and finely sliced zest of 1 lemon
2 tbsp gin
3–6 juniper berries, lightly crushed

Filling
2 eggs
150 ml cream
⅓ cup caster sugar
zest of 1 lemon, finely grated
100 ml lemon juice
2 tbsp gin

1   To make the pastry, process the flour and sugar in a food processor until well combined. Add zest and butter and process to fine crumbs. Add egg and tonic water and process until clumps form. Press together to form a ball, wrap in plastic wrap and chill for 30 minutes.

2   Preheat oven to 180°C. Grease a 23–25 cm loose-bottomed tart tin.

3   Roll pastry out on a lightly floured bench until it's big enough to line the tin (or is about 4 mm thick). Line the tin with the pastry. Prick the pastry all over with a fork, then chill for another 15 minutes.

4   Blind bake the tart (see Baker's Note on page 173) for 15 minutes, remove weights and bake for an additional 5–10 minutes or until bottom has dried out and edges are starting to colour. Set aside in tin on a wire rack.

5   To make the filling, whisk together all ingredients until well combined. Pour over cooked base.

6   Bake for 10–15 minutes or until filling is just set. Watch carefully after the 10-minute mark to ensure you don't overcook the tart. Cool on a wire rack.

7   To make the syrup, combine sugar, tonic water and lemon juice and place over a low heat. Stir until sugar is dissolved, then add zest, gin and juniper berries. Boil for 10 minutes.

8   To serve, pour some of the syrup over the tart, slice and serve with extra syrup.

Baker's Note — Blind Baking Pastry

When recipes ask you to 'blind bake' pastry they're telling you that you need to bake the shell by itself first. To do this, line your tin with pastry and chill for 15 minutes. Cover the bottom and sides of your chilled pastry with a piece of baking paper and fill with uncooked rice or beans (or ceramic pie weights). Bake for the specified time, then remove the baking paper and weights and return the pastry to the oven for the second specified time.

Rice or beans are a cheap option for weights and they can be used multiple times. I have a container of rice labelled *Baking weights* so that it doesn't inadvertently get cooked.

If you're blind baking small pies or tarts, rather than having to cut out circles of baking paper, use a cupcake case as a liner.

Raspberry Macaron *Cake*

This giant macaron is a lovely, light and incredibly tasty dessert. Make the macaron rounds up to two days in advance (store in an airtight container) and assemble just before serving. (See page 94 for the finer points of macaron-making.)

Serves 4–6

1½ cups ground almonds
1¾ cups icing sugar
¼ cup freeze-dried raspberry powder
4 egg whites
½ cup caster sugar
a few drops of pink food colouring

Balsamic Reduction
½ cup balsamic vinegar
2 tbsp sugar (optional)

Filling
500 ml cream
1 cup raspberries, fresh or frozen and thawed

1. Preheat oven to 150°C. Line three baking trays with baking paper. On one tray draw a 20 cm circle. On the other two trays draw a 20 cm circle with a 10 cm circle centred inside it (like a doughnut).

2. In a food processor, blend almonds, icing sugar and raspberry powder for 30 seconds or so.

3. Beat egg whites until stiff, then add caster sugar, one tablespoon at a time, beating very well after each addition. If you want a strong colour, beat in a few drops of food colouring (the freeze-dried powder will only lend a hint of colour).

4. Fold almond mixture into egg whites in three lots. Keep folding until a thick ribbon falls from your spatula when you hold it up.

5. Fill a piping bag and cut the bottom off so you have a 1.5–2 cm opening. Pipe the mixture to fill in the full circle and create the rings you've drawn (don't pipe inside the smaller circle) and set aside for 30–45 minutes. The macarons are ready to bake when you can touch them lightly without the batter sticking to your fingers.

6. Bake the trays, one at a time, for 10–15 minutes, removing when the edges start to colour. Once cooked, leave on the trays to cool before peeling off baking paper and storing in an airtight container.

7. To make the balsamic reduction, place vinegar and sugar (if using) into a small pot and simmer until reduced by at least half. Pour into a small dish to cool.

8 When you're ready to assemble the cake, whip the cream to form soft peaks.

9 Put the solid circle on your serving plate and top with half of the whipped cream. Place a ring on top and fill the open centre with raspberries. Smother the ring with the rest of the cream, top with the last ring and fill the centre with raspberries. Drizzle over 2–3 tbsp balsamic glaze and serve.

Baker's Note — Freeze-dried Fruit Powder

Freeze-dried fruit has been around for some time but now you can also get it in powder form which really adds a huge kick of flavour to your baking and desserts. I use the Fresh-As brand of freeze-dried fruit and fruit powder, which is an innovative range made here in New Zealand.

Goat's Cheese and Fig
Cheesecakes

Goat's cheese can have quite a strong flavour but here it's nicely balanced by the sweetness of the figs. Use a good-quality, flavoursome fig fruit paste in the cheesecake mix — I use Rutherford & Meyer, which I get from my local supermarket.

Makes 4 cheesecakes

Base
80 g plain sweet biscuits
60 g butter, melted

Cheesecake
250 g goat's cheese, at room temperature
250 g cream cheese, at room temperature
½ cup sweetened condensed milk
¼ cup cream
1½ tsp vanilla extract
120 g fig fruit paste

Fig Topping
½ cup boiling water
1 tbsp sugar
4 dried figs, chopped

½ cup toasted walnuts, chopped

1   In a food processor, whizz biscuits to a fine crumb. Alternatively, place biscuits in a sealable bag and crush with a rolling pin. Mix together biscuit crumbs and melted butter. Divide equally between four clean jars or individual ramekins (½ cup capacity) and press down (not too hard or it'll be difficult to eat).

2   In the bowl of a stand mixer, beat together goat's cheese and cream cheese until well combined and smooth. With the mixer on low, pour in condensed milk, cream and vanilla and beat until smooth.

3   Stir the fig fruit paste with a fork to loosen it up, then fold into cheese mixture. Spoon into jars and put in the fridge to set.

4   To make the fig topping, place water and sugar in a small bowl and stir together until sugar dissolves. Stir in figs and leave to soak for 10–20 minutes.

5   Spoon figs and syrup over cheesecakes and top with walnuts.

Baker's Note — Desserts in Jars
Desserts in jars are a great way to turn an otherwise impossible dessert into a portable, practical, delicious addition to a picnic or barbecue. You can serve almost any dessert in a jar, and you can even bake small portions of your favourite cakes directly in them (just check that your jars will take the heat by first filling them with water and baking as per the recipe you're using).

Turkish Delight
Semifreddo

Semifreddo means 'partially frozen' and is an Italian dessert. It doesn't involve having to churn ice cream or make custard, it can be made well in advance and makes a lovely end to a summer meal. Source good-quality, traditional Turkish Delight for the recipe — the stuff covered in chocolate just won't do!

Serves 8–10

¾ cup cream
2 eggs
⅓ cup caster sugar
2 tsp rosewater
¼ cup pistachios, toasted

¼ cup slivered almonds
1 cup raspberries, frozen or fresh
100 g good-quality rose-flavoured Turkish Delight
3 tbsp pistachios, to decorate

1 Line a 22 cm x 11 cm loaf tin with two layers of plastic wrap, leaving a 10 cm overhang on all sides.

2 Beat cream to soft peaks.

3 In another bowl, beat eggs and sugar until fluffy, then whisk or beat continuously over a pot of simmering water for another 5 minutes. Eggs should be thick, pale and fluffy.

4 Remove eggs from heat and whisk or beat again for another few minutes, then set aside to cool.

5 Fold one-third of the cream into the cool eggs to loosen the mixture. Fold in remaining cream, rosewater, pistachios, almonds and raspberries.

6 Place a layer of Turkish Delight in the bottom of your prepared loaf tin (depending on its thickness you may need to cut the Turkish Delight in half). Spoon in semifreddo. Cover with plastic wrap and freeze overnight.

7 Remove semifreddo from freezer 10 minutes before serving. Use the overhang of the plastic wrap to lift the semifreddo out of the tin. Turn it upside down, remove plastic wrap and top with pistachios. Use a sharp knife to cut into slices and serve immediately.

Variations
This is a great basic semifreddo recipe that easily lends itself to other flavour combinations. Try replacing the Turkish Delight, rosewater, raspberries and pistachios with the following:
• white chocolate, toasted hazelnuts and strawberries
• the zest of 1 orange, good-quality dark chocolate and freeze-dried mandarins
• dried fruit soaked in brandy, toasted almonds and ½ tsp ground cinnamon for a Christmassy flavour.

Rose and Buttermilk
Panna Cotta

Panna cotta is a wonderful creamy cooked custard that is brought to a whole new level with the inclusion of tart buttermilk. The buttermilk helps balance the sweetness of the rosewater and lychees and makes this dessert a delight to behold and eat.

Serves 4–6

2 tbsp cold water
4 tsp powdered gelatine
1 cup cream
½ cup caster sugar
3 tsp vanilla extract
¼ tsp salt
2 cups buttermilk, at room temperature
3 tsp rosewater

Topping

1 x 425 g can lychees in syrup
½ cup raspberries
rose petals, to decorate (optional)

1   Put the water in a small bowl and sprinkle over the gelatine. Stir briskly with a fork to combine and set aside.

2   In a heavy-based saucepan over a medium heat, bring cream, sugar, vanilla and salt to a simmer. Whisk in gelatine, buttermilk and rosewater until smooth.

3   Divide between 4–6 clean, dry moulds or ramekins (½ cup capacity) and refrigerate for at least 3 hours, preferably overnight.

4   Ten minutes before you're ready to serve, combine lychees and raspberries and set aside.

5   Unmould panna cotta by wrapping a hot cloth around the outside and base of the mould (you may also need to run a small knife around the edge) and invert onto a serving plate. Top with lychees and raspberries and a drizzle of the syrup. Decorate with rose petals, if wished.

Baker's Note — Boiling Cream or Milk
Be careful not to let the cream boil when it's on the stove top as, if it does, it may split or curdle. If this happens, the only thing you can do is start again with a fresh pot of cream or you may find that your panna cotta separates as it cools.

Quinoa Pudding with
Orange Blossom Apricots

If you're a fan of rice pudding, you'll love quinoa pudding. The best thing about quinoa (see Baker's Note below) is that it doesn't go mushy like rice pudding so it's difficult to overcook. If you've never used (or even heard of) quinoa, then you're in for a treat — it's nutty, slightly crunchy and full of goodness so this is a healthy dessert, really. Honest.

Serves 4

¾ cup quinoa
2 cups milk (full cream is best)
1 cup cream
¼ cup caster sugar
1 tsp ground cardamom
1 tsp ground cinnamon

Orange Blossom Apricots
1 cup dried apricots
2 cups water
zest of 1 lime, finely grated
¼ cup caster sugar
1½ tsp orange blossom water
3 tbsp pistachios, to serve

1   Place quinoa in a sieve and rinse under running water for 30 seconds.

2   In a medium heavy-based saucepan, put milk, cream, sugar, cardamom and cinnamon. Bring to a simmer over a medium heat, then add quinoa.

3   Reduce heat to low and simmer for 45 minutes or until a thick, soupy consistency is reached (it will thicken a bit more as it cools). Cool to room temperature. Cover and place in fridge until cold.

4   To make orange blossom apricots, place apricots, water, lime zest and sugar in a small pot and bring to a simmer. Simmer until apricots are soft (about 20 minutes). Remove from heat and stir in orange blossom water.

5   To serve, spoon quinoa into serving bowls and top with apricots and syrup and a sprinkle of pistachios.

Baker's Note — Quinoa

Quinoa (pronounced *keen-wa*) is a South American grain that can replace rice in most dishes (it's delicious instead of rice in a salad). You can find it in the supermarket, shelved with rice or with the organic foods.

Honey Panna Cotta with

Plum Jelly

Silky-smooth panna cotta and tart jelly make for a grown-up version of jelly and ice cream. Use whatever glass jars, glasses or bowls you have on hand to make these in (glass shows off the layers), or make in small pudding moulds and turn out onto plates to serve.

Serves 4–6

¼ cup water
2¼ tsp powdered gelatine
2 cups cream
2 tsp vanilla extract
⅓ cup honey
⅓ cup sugar
1 tbsp lemon juice
1 cup buttermilk or Greek yoghurt

Plum Jelly

3 cups water
4 tsp powdered gelatine
⅔ cup sugar
40 g freeze-dried plum powder

freeze-dried plums, to decorate

1 Place 4–6 jars, moulds, cups or glasses (whatever you're going to set the dessert in) into the fridge to chill.

2 To make the panna cotta, put the water in a small bowl and sprinkle over the gelatine. Stir well with a fork and set aside.

3 Place the cream, vanilla extract, honey and sugar in a heavy-based saucepan and bring to a simmer over a medium heat.

4 Remove from heat and stir in gelatine until smooth. Stir in lemon juice and buttermilk or Greek yoghurt and set aside to cool to room temperature.

5 To make plum jelly, put ¼ cup water in a small bowl and sprinkle over the gelatine. Stir well with a fork and set aside.

6 Add the remaining water and the sugar to a small pot and bring to the boil, stirring to dissolve the sugar.

7 Stir in the gelatine and plum powder until smooth. Set aside to cool slightly.

8 To layer desserts, pour a small amount of jelly into the base of the chilled serving dishes, then place in the fridge until the jelly is set. It's best to use a measuring cup to make the layers even.

9 Once set, pour an equal amount of panna cotta over the jelly and return to the fridge to set. Continue until your serving dishes are full.

10 Remove from fridge 10 minutes or so before serving to warm them up a little. Top with freeze-dried plum pieces and serve.

Variations

This dessert can be varied in many ways. Change the flavour of the jelly. Add chopped fruit to the jelly. Use a packet jelly instead of making your own with freeze-dried powder and make to packet instructions (go easy on the sugar in the panna cotta if you do this, or it will be too sweet). Remove the honey from the panna cotta, replace with more sugar and flavour with melted chocolate, cocoa or citrus zest.

Matcha Green Tea
Sponge Roll

Matcha green tea is made in Japan by grinding green tea leaves to a very fine powder. So fine, in fact, that it dissolves in hot water. The wonderful thing about green tea in baking is that it takes away some of the sweetness of the finished product and brings a wonderful depth of flavour.

Serves 8–10

3 eggs
½ cup caster sugar
½ cup plain flour
1 tsp baking powder
2 tbsp matcha green tea powder

Raspberry Cream
300 ml cream
1 cup raspberries, fresh or frozen and thawed

icing sugar, for dusting

1   Preheat oven to 200°C. Spray and line a Swiss roll tin with baking paper, leaving an overhang of about 7 cm at each end.

2   Beat eggs and sugar until light, fluffy and pale (at least 5 minutes).

3   Sift flour, baking powder and tea into a small bowl, then sift again to get more air into it. Fold into beaten eggs.

4   Spread batter evenly over the base of the prepared tin.

5   Bake for 10 minutes or until it starts to pull away from the sides.

6   While it's cooking, sprinkle a large piece of baking paper lightly with icing sugar and, when the roll is cooked, immediately turn it out onto the clean baking paper and peel off the baking paper it was cooked on. Roll up along the short edge, place seam-side down and set aside to cool.

7   To make the raspberry cream, whip the cream to medium peaks, then fold in the raspberries. Use the back of a spoon to crush some of the berries.

8   When roll is cold, carefully unroll and fill with raspberry cream. Re-roll and place seam side-down on a serving plate. Dust lightly with icing sugar and serve.

Baker's Note — Matcha Green Tea

Matcha green tea, apart from being delicious to drink, can be used in a number of ways in your baking. For a delicious twist on old favourites try adding it to macarons, plain muffins, Madeira cake or even to ice cream. It can be found in some Asian supermarkets or in specialty tea stores. I buy mine online from t leaf T.

Neapolitan
Layer Cake

This cake can be made in any colour configuration you wish. Let your imagination and taste buds take flight and don't be limited by the recipes as they are written. Experiment with different flavours, too. The white cake (see page 60) is a great base for pretty much any colour or flavour you care to add.

Serves 12–14

1 recipe White Cake batter (see page 60)
pink food colouring
1½ tsp strawberry essence (optional)
½ recipe Nanny's Chocolate Cake batter (see page 69)
2 recipes buttercream icing (see page 36)
1 cup strawberry or raspberry jam (see page 46)

Simple Chocolate Icing
2 cups icing sugar
½ cup cocoa
2 tbsp butter, softened
hot water

Pink and white layers

1 Preheat oven to 180°C. Grease and line two 23 cm round tins.

2 Make one recipe of White Cake (see page 60). When you get to Step 5, divide the batter into two equal portions (use a scale to ensure they weigh the same). Colour one half with pink food colouring and add essence, if desired.

3 Pour each batter into a prepared tin.

4 Bake for 20–25 minutes or until a skewer inserted comes out with a few crumbs on it.

5 Cool the cake in the tins for 10 minutes before turning out onto a wire rack to cool completely.

Chocolate layer

1 Preheat oven to 170°C. Grease and line a 23 cm round tin.

2 Make a half recipe of Nanny's Chocolate Cake (see page 69).

3 Bake for 20–25 minutes or until a skewer inserted comes out with a few crumbs on it.

4 Cool the cake in the tins for 10 minutes before turning out onto a wire rack to cool completely.

Buttercream

1 Make a double recipe of buttercream icing (see page 36).

2 Place one-third of the icing into another bowl and colour it with pink food colouring. Strawberry essence may be added, if desired.

Simple Chocolate Icing

1. Sift icing sugar and cocoa into a bowl. Add butter and 2 tbsp hot water.
2. Stir well and add more hot water, a tablespoon at a time, until you reach a thick icing that almost plops off your spoon.

Assembling the cake

1. Place 1 tbsp white buttercream on your cake board and spread around. Place the chocolate cake directly onto this.
2. Spread the chocolate layer with ½ cup jam, then ½ cup buttercream.
3. Place the pink layer on top and repeat with jam and buttercream. Put the white layer on the top, then put the cake in the fridge for 30 minutes to chill.
4. Once the cake is chilled, apply a crumb coat. To do this, use a small amount of white buttercream (no more than 1 cup) to thinly coat the cake on the sides and top (see page 159).
5. Chill the cake for another 30 minutes.
6. Using a palette knife or offset spatula, apply the pink buttercream to the bottom half of the sides of the cake, smoothing it out as you go.
7. Use the remaining white buttercream to ice the rest of the cake (including the top).
8. Blend the pink and white buttercreams together gently so that you don't get a sharp line. Leave the icing to set for about 30 minutes.
9. Stir your chocolate icing well (you may need to add more hot water if it is too stiff) and, using a palette knife, ice the top of the cake. Encourage the chocolate icing to ooze over the sides of the cake a bit.
10. To get the spiral pattern on top of the cake, start in the middle, with your palette knife at a 45-degree angle, and turn the cake (not your hand!), slowly dragging your knife out from the centre as you turn.
11. Transfer cake to a pretty cake stand and enjoy!

Celebration Cake

Nothing says celebration like a multi-layered cake slathered in creamy delicious Swiss meringue buttercream. Here, I've finished the cake in delicate shades of pink and topped it with tiny baby booties — perfect for a christening or naming day, or even a baby shower.

Serves 12–16

2 recipes Nanny's Chocolate Cake (see page 69)
2 recipes Swiss meringue buttercream (see page 146), flavoured and coloured
jam, curd or ganache (see page 140), for inside the cake (optional)
sprinkles, icing decorations, ribbon or flowers, to decorate

1   Preheat oven to 170°C. Grease and line three 23 cm round tins.

2   Make a double recipe of Nanny's Chocolate Cake (see page 69). Divide it equally between the three prepared tins.

3   Bake each cake for 30–40 minutes or until a skewer inserted in the middle comes out with a few crumbs on it.

4   Make a double recipe of Swiss meringue buttercream (see page 146) and flavour and colour it as you wish. Here, I've used strawberry essence and pink colouring.

5   To assemble the cake, follow the instructions on page 158. Use jam, curd or ganache on the inside layers, if you wish.

6   Slide onto a serving platter or dish before topping with sprinkles and/or other decorations.

Baker's Note — Sprinkles and Cake Toppers
There is an amazing array of sprinkles, cake toppers and decorations available from cake decorating supply stores, craft shops and even your local supermarket. It doesn't take much to make your finished cake look fantastic — even a few fresh flowers tied in a simple posy can do the trick. Have fun and let your imagination take flight.

Hints and Tips for the Home Baker

Ingredients

Butter

As unsalted butter isn't the most common of ingredients in the average home kitchen, I use salted butter in all my recipes. If your preference is for unsalted, you may need to add more salt to the recipe to get a balanced flavour.

Buttermilk

I use buttermilk in quite a few recipes because it adds a lovely lightness to baking. Buttermilk keeps a long time in the fridge (up to three weeks after its use-by date, I've discovered) so if you don't use it all at once, don't panic. If you haven't got any buttermilk, you can find suggestions for alternatives on page 29.

Chocolate

Unless the recipe suggests otherwise, try to use chocolate with at least 60 per cent cocoa solids. Anything less will definitely impact upon the flavour. I use Pams as it is 60 per cent (unlike the 'name' brands which are 40 per cent) or Whittaker's (for 72 per cent and white chocolate).

Cocoa

I use natural unsweetened cocoa powder (not Dutch process cocoa powder) because that is what is most readily available in supermarkets. Because the process of making Dutch cocoa involves treating it with an alkaline (which removes the acid), it won't react the same as natural unsweetened cocoa in recipes, therefore they are not interchangeable.

Eggs

All recipes in this book use size seven eggs (also known as 'large eggs'). I also recommend you use barn-raised or free-range eggs as they have a much better flavour and are produced ethically. Eggs should always be at room temperature for baking. A size seven egg is 62 grams and a size seven egg white is 35 ml.

Flour

I use plain flour for cakes, biscuits, cupcakes, slices, etc. and high grade for bread and pastry. High grade flour is 'stronger' as it has more protein (gluten).

How to measure flour by cup

The most accurate way to measure flour when using cups is to use the 'spoon and sweep' method. Start by giving your flour a bit of a stir in its container, then use a spoon or scoop to fill up your measuring cup until it is overfull. Then use a knife or the back of your finger to sweep off the excess. Never, ever tap the flour down or press it into the cup. Try to avoid filling your measuring cup by scooping it directly into your flour — it won't be accurate enough as it will pack the flour in too tightly.

Sugar

Brown sugar
All brown sugar measurements in this book refer to a 'firmly packed' cup, i.e. press the brown sugar into the measuring cup until it is full.

Caster sugar
I use caster sugar quite often for my baking, especially when creaming butter and sugar is required as it dissolves more easily than regular white sugar. If you haven't got caster sugar, you can substitute standard sugar — you will just need to beat it for longer.

Vanilla
Vanilla is an important ingredient in baking. Like salt, it's not something you can taste in most baking but if it's missing, you'll definitely know it! I specify vanilla extract in all my recipes as it's an economical way to get a real vanilla flavour. If you prefer, you can use vanilla paste (about ½ tsp paste equals 1 tsp extract) or vanilla bean (scraped seeds or soak the whole pod if making desserts with milk). Where extract comes from the actual vanilla pod, essence is made from chemicals and really is an inferior product.

Yeast
I use bread maker yeast because I find it more reliable and easier to use than active dried yeast. If you'd prefer to use active dried yeast, you will need to 'activate' it with a small amount of warm liquid, according to the package's instructions, before it is added to the other ingredients. Add 1.25 times the amount of bread maker yeast, if you're using active dried. If you're lucky enough to be able to get fresh yeast, multiply the bread maker yeast measurement by 1.4 to get the correct amount to add to your recipe.

Baking Essentials

Baking your goods
The best place to put your cake tin or baking tray is on a rack in the middle of the oven. You can bake more than one tray or cake at a time (unless the recipe specifically says not to) by placing them in the upper and lower thirds of the oven. To ensure even cooking, rotate the trays or cakes when they are just over halfway through cooking.

Creaming butter
Creaming butter and sugar is an important process and shouldn't be cut short as it adds much-needed air into your baking, making your finished product light and airy. Generally, creaming with a stand

mixer or an electric hand beater will take 5–10 minutes. It can take up to 20 minutes, if you're doing it by hand! The general rule of thumb is that the mix is properly creamed when all the sugar has dissolved and it is at least the colour of lightly whipped cream (if not lighter). If there is any hint of yellow, keep going!

Decorating cakes

When you're decorating cakes and you want a perfect finish, I highly recommend chilling your cake before you apply the icing. Not only will this result in a nice smooth finish but it will also stop crumbs coming through the icing as you smear it around.

Disposable piping bags

I use disposable piping bags for all my piping. Not only do they make cleaning up a breeze, but they also allow you to store icing away from the air, which stops it hardening. You can buy disposable piping bags from cake decorating supply stores and from some supermarkets. They're usually found in the same place as cupcake cases.

Filling the tin

Once you've combined your wet and dry ingredients, it's important that you get your tin in the oven as soon as possible. This is because the raising agent (baking powder or baking soda) starts reacting as soon as it gets wet and the longer you leave it, the less time the rising agent will have to work in the oven.

Latent heat

Always remove your baking from the tin at the end of the cooling time specified in the recipe. This is because the latent heat remaining in the tin will continue to cook your baking even though it's out of the oven. This is especially important for cupcakes and muffins because of their small size.

Ovens

Ovens vary (sometimes greatly) so it's important that you consider the times given in recipes as guidelines only and check your baking often to ensure even cooking.

All the recipes in this book have been baked using a fan-forced oven. If your oven doesn't have a fan-forced option, you will need to increase the temperature, and maybe cook the item for a bit longer, too.

The age of your oven may affect how things bake. You may have hot spots or cool spots or it may be that it no longer heats to the correct temperature. If this is the case, the best thing you can invest in is an oven thermometer. You can get them from kitchen shops and they can really save your bakin'!

Preparing your tin

Greasing and lining your tins properly means you won't have to argue with your baked goods when it comes time to unmould them.

Grease well with melted butter or spray with oil, and line with baking paper if the recipe indicates it. Always allow a little overhanging baking paper as it helps when you're lifting your cake or slice out of the tin.

If the recipe calls for you to 'grease and flour' your tin, brush the sides well with melted butter or spray with oil, getting into all the nooks and crannies. Sprinkle over a generous tablespoon of flour (or cocoa, if it's a dark-coloured cake) and rotate the tin while shaking it to evenly disperse the flour over the grease. Tap the bottom and sides of the tin lightly upside-down over the sink to remove any excess flour.

Storage

Most baked items should be stored in an airtight container.

If you've baked cakes and they're not cool enough to put in containers for overnight storage, then place a piece of bread on top of the middle of the cake. The bread will dry out and the cake won't.

The right-sized tin

Using the tin size specified in the recipe is very important. If you overfill the tin because it's too small, you'll end up with a sticky mess on the bottom of your oven, cake down the sides of the tin and a sunken, collapsed cake, to boot. If you underfill the tin because it's too large, the cake will cook quicker and is more likely to burn and cook unevenly.

If you don't have the correct-sized tin to make a cake, the best thing to do is two-thirds fill it so it doesn't overflow (and discard the extra batter or use it to make cupcakes), or watch it like a hawk for the last 10–20 minutes if it's bigger than specified.

Conversion Tables

International measures

Although measuring spoons and cups may vary from New Zealand to Australia and also from Europe to North America, the difference does not generally significantly affect a recipe. Spoon and cup measurements should be level.

1 cup in New Zealand holds 250 ml (8 fl oz)
1 teaspoon holds 5 ml
1 tablespoon holds 15 ml (as in North America and the UK, although an Australian tablespoon holds 20 ml)

Liquids

Cup	Metric	Imperial
1 tbsp	15 ml	½ fl oz
⅛ cup	30 ml	1 fl oz
¼ cup	60 ml	2 fl oz
⅓ cup	80 ml	2½ fl oz
½ cup	125 ml	4 fl oz
⅔ cup	160 ml	5 fl oz
¾ cup	180 ml	6 fl oz
1 cup	250 ml	8 fl oz
2 cups	500 ml	16 fl oz
2¼ cups	560 ml	20 fl oz
4 cups	1 litre	32 fl oz

Solids

Metric	Imperial
15 g	½ oz
30 g	1 oz
60 g	2 oz
125 g	4 oz
180 g	6 oz
250 g	8 oz
500 g	16 oz (1 lb)
1 kg	32 oz (2 lb)

Celsius to Fahrenheit

Celsius	Fahrenheit
100°C	200°F
120°C	250°F
140°C	275°F
150°C	300°F
160°C	325°F
180°C	350°F
190°C	375°F
200°C	400°F
220°C	425°F

Millimetres to inches

Metric	Imperial
3 mm	⅛ inch
6 mm	¼ inch
1 cm	½ inch
2.5 cm	1 inch
5 cm	2 inches
18 cm	7 inches
20 cm	8 inches
23 cm	9 inches
25 cm	10 inches
30 cm	12 inches

Electric to gas

Celsius	Gas
110°C	¼
130°C	½
140°C	1
150°C	2
170°C	3
180°C	4
190°C	5
200°C	6
220°C	7
230°C	8
240°C	9
250°C	10

Substitutions

Substituting one ingredient for another is a great way to adapt a recipe if you find you've run out of something. The two main ingredients that home bakers often think about substituting are fat (butter/oil) and sweeteners (sugar/honey/maple syrup). Unfortunately, these two ingredients play an important role in the texture, volume, moisture and flavour of the final product.

Fats

If your recipe requires you to cream butter and sugar, simply swapping the butter for vegetable oil or fruit purée will not work as creaming beats much-needed air into a batter, helping it rise. One way to counteract this is to fold beaten egg whites into your batter (as they are full of bubbles). Another is to add more raising agent (baking powder or soda), but beware that adding too much will result in an unpleasant flavour.

If your recipe calls for melted butter, substitute away to your heart's content. It will affect the final texture and flavour, but not the rise in any great way. You can also try replacing part of the butter with oil (start with replacing one-third and go from there). This can work with some biscuits.

Sweeteners

Sugar adds tenderness, moisture and flavour to baking. One type of sugar can easily be swapped for another on a 1:1 ratio, but you may need to decrease the liquids elsewhere in the recipe if you use honey or another liquid sweetener. Artificial sweeteners should be substituted as per the manufacturer's instructions.

Common Substitutes

Ingredient	Amount	Substitutions
Baking powder	1 tsp	¼ tsp baking soda + ½ tsp cream of tartar
Butter	100 g	100 g full-fat margarine; or 75 ml vegetable oil + ½ tsp salt; or 100 ml olive oil + ½ tsp salt; or 100 ml apple sauce or other fruit purée
Cornflour	1 tsp	1 tbsp flour; or 1 tsp arrowroot powder
Cream (liquid)	1 cup	1 cup evaporated milk; or ¾ cup milk + ⅓ cup melted butter
Egg	1 whole	2 egg yolks; or 2 egg whites; or half a banana mashed with ½ tsp baking powder; or ⅓ cup fruit purée (e.g. apple sauce) and ½ tsp baking powder
Flour (plain)	1 cup	1 cup high-grade flour less 2 tbsp; or 1 cup self-raising flour (remove 1½ tsp baking powder and ½ tsp salt from recipe); or 1 cup of wholemeal flour*
Flour (self-raising)	1 cup	1 cup plain flour + 1½ tsp baking powder and ½ tsp of salt
Gelatine (powdered)	1 tbsp	2 sheets/leaves; or 1 tbsp agar agar flakes; or 1 tsp powdered agar agar
Golden syrup	1 tbsp	1 tbsp treacle; or 1 tbsp molasses; or 1 tbsp maple syrup; or 1 tbsp corn syrup
Honey	1 cup	1 cup and 2 tbsp sugar + ¼ cup of the same liquid used in recipe
Milk	1 cup	1 cup soy/rice/almond milk; or ⅔ cup evaporated milk + ⅓ cup water
Oil (vegetable)	1 cup	1 cup apple sauce/fruit purée; or 1 cup olive oil; or 250 g melted butter
Sour cream	1 cup	1 cup plain unsweetened yoghurt; or 1 tbsp lemon juice or vinegar + enough cream to make 1 cup

* Note: Substitute wholemeal flour for plain at a 1:1 ratio, remembering, though, that wholemeal flour will will make baked goods denser. Using a combination of plain and wholemeal flour will produce a lighter result.

Acknowledgements

To all my friends, thank you for your support and enthusiasm during the long book-baking process. Not only did you all unselfishly take test baking off my hands (for which I am very grateful) and give me feedback where required, you also put up with my cancelling things at the last minute, dropping the ball on various committee requirements and even took Isobel off my hands when I was desperate. Thank you, ladies — you were amazing!

To the local Martinborough-ites who enthusiastically supported me through the TV show and have continued to do so through this new challenge. The lovely chefs and owners of the Village Café, Café Medici and Providore Food and Catering who kindly provided me with the secrets to my favourites of their baked goods; the cheerful crowd at P&K who always asked how the book was going and how long until they could get one; and the wonderfully supportive Sue, owner of my local kitchen store Mint @ Martinborough. Sue not only supplied beautiful kitchenware, but also the amazing bracelets shown gracing the cover.

Thank you to Anthea Lawrence of Anthea Lawrence Design who not only provided the beautiful dresses I wear, but also the amazing Tilli jars featured in the Cheat's Chocolate Trifle (see page 74).

Thank you also to the very talented Josephine Durkin of Oggi Domani Ceramics. She kindly lent me some of her amazing hand-painted Italian ware for the Village Café's Hummingbird Cake (see page 70) and the Quinoa Pudding (see page 183).

This book wouldn't be nearly as pretty without the incredible generosity of Daphne Geisler from Gertrude Snyder's Vintage Treasure in Martinborough. Not only did she let me borrow anything I wished from her store, but she also let me rummage through her garage and her prized possessions at home. Her boundless enthusiasm and endless supply of beautiful antiques made styling this book a dream. Thank you, Daphne, I couldn't have done it without you.

To my mother-in-law Lorraine, who not only sold me on her son but then went on to sell me to the lovely people at HarperCollins — two life-changing events which make her the best mother-in-law ever. She also stepped in during the school holidays to corral Isobel, for which I'm very grateful.

To the wonderful and talented team at HarperCollins; the publicists, marketers, sales reps, accountants, warehouse staff and everyone else — thank you for your hard work and dedication. Thank you especially to Vicki Marsdon for believing in me and fighting for my cause, Antoinette Sturny for correcting all my mistakes, and the incredibly talented Cheryl Rowe for making both my blog and this book look so beautiful.

To my wonderful photographer Murray Lloyd. Not only are you an amazingly talented photographer who can make even the shoddiest styling look good, but you are also incredibly kind and generous with your expertise (as well as patient when the toddler interrupted). I've so enjoyed working with you on this project. Thank you.

To the three women who taught me to bake: my mum Shelley, my grandmother Valerie, and my fifth form Home Economics teacher Miss Barbara Englebretson. You all instilled in me a love for baking that shines in these pages and I hope you're proud of what you produced!

And, finally, to my wonderful husband Shane and beautiful daughter Isobel. Thank you for putting up with a messy house (and an even messier kitchen) during the development stage, a living room that looked like a garage sale during the photography stage, and the stress and distraction during the writing stage. Thank you for encouraging me when I was down, nagging me when I was slow and always supporting me no matter what. I love you both.

This book would not have been possible without the generous support of the following:

Katie and Jeff Yates at New World, Carterton

Gertrude Snyder Vintage Treasure

Mint @ Martinborough

Anthea Lawrence Design

Oggi Domani Ceramics

The Village Café

Café Medici

Providore Food and Catering

Martinborough Vineyard (www.martinborough-vineyard.co.nz)

Renaissance Brewing (www.renaissancebrewing.co.nz)

t Leaf T (www.tleaft.co.nz)

Jessica Design Store (www.jessicandesign.com)

Index

Alice Arndell

Inspiring, self-taught home baker Alice Arndell was introduced to the art of baking by her mother and grandmother and to the science of baking by her high school Home Economics teacher. Both art and science combine in Alice's baking and her emphasis on creating 'home baking for home bakers' means that no matter your level of expertise, you too can create amazing, flavoursome 'cakes and bakes', using supermarket ingredients and basic equipment.

A finalist in Season Three of television's *Chelsea New Zealand's Hottest Home Baker*, Alice now runs her own inspirational blog 'Alice in Bakingland' and writes for food publications.

Murray Lloyd

Murray Lloyd is a freelance photographer and photography lecturer based in Wellington. He has a passion for eating, cooking and photographing food. Previous books include *Ruth Pretty Entertains, The Ruth Pretty Cookbook, Ruth Pretty Cooking at Springfield, Ruth Pretty's Favourite Recipes, Ruth Pretty at Home* and *A Consuming Passion* by Adam Newell. Murray writes a blog themed around food-related topics and photographs food for a wide range of commercial clients and publications in New Zealand and abroad.

His work can be seen at www.murraylloyd.com.